THE WORD OF MOUTH ON
WORD OF MOUTH MARKETING

"A quick, practical, and extremely useful guide to word of mouth marketing."
— **Emanuel Rosen, author of** *The Anatomy of Buzz*

"This book is to Gladwell's *The Tipping Point* as Engineering is to Physics. If you want to understand the deep sociological theories behind interpersonal communication, this isn't the book for you. If you want to understand how to harness interpersonal communication to drive your business, then buy this book."
— **David Godes, Associate Professor, Harvard Business School**

"Word of mouth is the valuable currency in today's advertising-saturated world. Andy Sernovitz has written a book packed with ideas on how to do word of mouth marketing the right way."
— **Jackie Huba and Ben McConnell,**
authors of *Creating Customer Evangelists*

"It's brief. It's elementary. It's obvious. But the truth often is. Read this book to relearn what you always knew just in time for it to change your business life."
— **Bob Garfield, Co-Host of NPR's** *On The Media*

"A primer chock-full of great stories, tips, and exercises to make you a better word of mouth marketer, no matter what size company you work for. Read it, and you will increase your influence with your customers, and make yourself more influential in your company."
— **Ed Keller and Jon Berry, The Keller Fay Group,**
authors of *The Influentials*

"It's an actionable guide for anyone looking to capture the power of word of mouth. Andy has written a book that shows just how simple it is to get people talking about your business. You should read this book and then tell a friend."
— **Brad Santeler, Director, Kimberly-Clark**

"No one knows word of mouth (the good, the bad, and the measurable) better than Andy Sernovitz."
— **Peter Fader, Professor, Wharton School of Business**

"The coolest book on the hottest topic in marketing and communication. Andy tells it all and tells it like it really is. The Five Ts are the best organizing framework for word of mouth I have seen yet. Use them and profit. No hype. No smoke and mirrors. No overblown promises."
— **Don E. Schultz, Professor Emeritus-in-Service, Northwestern University**

"There is no wasted word in this practical guide. Pure nuts-and-bolts how-tos for people who want to start implementing a word of mouth marketing program today. Other books cover the theory, but Andy gets to the actual action best."
— **George Silverman, author of** *The Secrets of Word-of-Mouth Marketing*

"Andy Sernovitz's book will give all marketers a reason to talk. Sernovitz not only legitimizes word of mouth marketing, he provides THE roadmap to what drives it."
— **MaryLee Sachs, Chairman, US, Hill & Knowlton, Inc.**

"As I read through *Word of Mouth Marketing* I felt, more than anything else, relieved. Relieved that we finally have a marketing author who understands the simplicity (and complexity) of this business; who recognizes that honesty is the only workable policy for advertisers; and who sees that in a flat, information-flooded world nothing but the right product—a product fashioned around your customers needs—will cut it. Sernovitz has managed to achieve a pretty rare two-fer in providing a simple, tactical, how-to guide that anyone could use to improve their communications efforts, while simultaneously sketching out a whole new philosophy for marketers and advertisers everywhere. Oh, and the guy has fun anecdotes and a readable style too. Seriously, I know you're bored silly by all those marketing texts, and I am too, but this one's worth your time."
— **Jonah Bloom, Executive Editor,** *Advertising Age*

"Another must-read if you're at all interested in word of mouth marketing."
— **Mark Hughes, author of *Buzzmarketing***

"Forget the overinflated hype that characterizes many business books. Andy has written a 'real world' guide."
— **Paul M. Rand, Partner, Global Chief Development and Innovation Officer, Ketchum**

"Andy's approach is practical, affordable and, best of all, ethical. Don't waste your money on mass marketing: Spend it on this book and start people talking."
— **Greg Steilstra, author of *PyroMarketing***

"There is a wrong way and a right way to market in a networked world. Andy lays out simple steps to ethical and effective messaging."
— **Shawn Gold, Senior Vice President, MySpace**

"Andy brings it together perfectly: the vision, the strategy, and the practical how-to. It's all here."
— **Geoff Ramsey, CEO, eMarketer**

WORD *of* MOUTH MARKETING

HOW SMART COMPANIES GET PEOPLE TALKING

ANDY SERNOVITZ

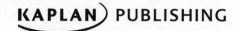

KAPLAN PUBLISHING

Vice President and Publisher: Maureen McMahon
Editorial Director: Jennifer Farthing
Acquisitions Editor: Karen Murphy
Production Editor: Caitlin Ostrow
Typesetter: Todd Bowman
Cover Designer: Jody Billert, Design Literate

Library of Congress Cataloging-in-Publication Data

Sernovitz, Andy.
    Word of mouth marketing : how smart companies get people talking /
Andy Sernovitz.
        p. cm.
    ISBN-13: 978-1-4195-9333-8
    ISBN-10: 1-4195-9333-1
1. Word-of-mouth advertising. I. Title.
    HF5827.95.S47 2006
    659.13'3—dc22

                                                                    2006024165

Kaplan Publishing books are available at special quantity discounts to use for sales promotions, employee premiums, or educational purposes. Please call our Special Sales Department to order or for more information at 800-621-9621, ext. 4444, e-mail kaplanpubsales@kaplan.com, or write to Kaplan Publishing, 30 South Wacker Drive, Suite 2500, Chicago, IL 60606-7481.

There is only one thing in the world worse than being talked about, and that is not being talked about.

—Oscar Wilde (*The Picture of Dorian Gray*)

Contents

A Note to the Reader   xi

Thank You   xv

Foreword by Seth Godin   xvii

Preface   xix

Introduction   xxiii

Part 1
The Essential Concepts

1. What Is Word of Mouth Marketing?   3

2. Deep Stuff: Six Big Ideas   39

3. The Word of Mouth Marketing Manifesto   59

Part 2
How to Do It—The Five Ts in Action

4. Talkers: Who Will Tell Their Friends About You?   65

5. Topics: What Will They Talk About?   95

6. Tools: How Can You Help the Message Travel?   117

7. Taking Part: How Can You Join the Conversation?   151

8. Tracking: What Are People Saying About You?   167

And in the End . . .

Sixteen Sure-Thing, Must-Do, Awfully Easy Word of Mouth Marketing Techniques   181

Choose to Be Good   182

Afterword: Yet Another Top 10 by Guy Kawasaki   183

A Note
to the Reader

How to Get Started

Read this book.

Then try a few of the simple suggestions. People will start talking about you in just a few days.

Then do a few of the more involved ideas. Even more people will start talking about you.

And when you have a chance, think about the philosophy behind word of mouth marketing (marked "Deep Stuff"). This is a little bit harder, not as immediate, but more important.

When these ideas jell, everyone will be talking about you. And they will respect your company. And they will like you better. And you'll like you and your company better.

And that is very cool.

The Great Word of Mouth Hyphen
Controversy of 2006

A brief aside for all the editors and strict grammarians reading this: Yes, I do know that *word of mouth* is supposed to be
hyphenated *word-of-mouth*. Actually, it's hyphenated when it's an
adjective—"word-of-mouth marketing"—and not when it's a
noun. But no one ever gets it right, so I'm going to skip the
hyphens. That's the advantage of being one of the first people
in a new industry—you get to define the terms.

Now that this is written, I am allowed to return home to my
wife, the professional editor, who still isn't happy about all of
this. But I hope she will settle for this note, as she graciously
accepts many far worse quirks.

Examples, Stories, and Data

This book is full of anecdotes, stories, and examples. They
are true but not always verifiable. I heard many of them through
word of mouth.

Also, you'll find almost no hard data, numbers, or statistics.
This was an intentional choice.

Many great books and resources provide detailed analysis
and data about the phenomena and trends discussed here.
Also, a robust word of mouth research industry produces
immense amounts of very useful data. (Much of it is available
free at *www.womma.org/research.*)

For our purposes in this book, however, it doesn't really matter. The point is to share examples that help you understand the
magic of word of mouth and stories that show how you can use
it for yourself. The specifics aren't as important as the lessons.

This book is about simple, actionable things you can do.
It's not a business case study or a textbook. It's the story of a
new kind of marketing that is easier, more effective, and more

accessible to the average businessperson. The numbers get in the way of telling that story.

More Information

Check out the website that goes with the book: *www.wordofmouthbook.com*. It's full of ideas, examples, and resources to help you master word of mouth. I'll also be testing and demonstrating a lot of the ideas that you read here.

Thank You

Everything I get credit for these days is really a synthesis of the generous work and clever ideas of hundreds of very smart people. I'm very lucky to be at the center of a trade association where all the greatest minds come together to make the future happen. I get to talk to them all day long, help where I can, and absorb neat, new things like a sponge. So let me specifically thank the members of the Word of Mouth Marketing Association for their thoughts and generosity—and for letting me be part of this exciting adventure.

My friend Peter Waldheim has spent more hours on the phone with me, helping me through both crises and craziness, than any rational person should, and I appreciate it more than I can express.

And of course, Julie Grisham, my wife and love, has been unreasonably supportive and selfless through a decade of entrepreneurial ups and downs and personal insanity. I am only able to do this because of her generosity, tolerance, and understanding. (Plus, she's an amazingly talented editor who has put a huge amount of time into making this book better than I ever could have.)

Foreword
by Seth Godin

People talk about Andy. Wherever he goes, whatever industry he's in, Andy Sernovitz causes a conversation.

That's his secret. Don't tell anyone (actually, go ahead—he won't mind). By causing a conversation, and then creating organizations that make it easy for the conversation to continue, Andy thrives. He is a living, breathing example of the power of word of mouth.

This isn't the first book on the topic (I wrote *Unleashing the Ideavirus* six years ago, and mine wasn't even the first). It probably won't be the last, either. But what this book offers you is two things: first, Andy's vision as honed through his work in the trenches, year after year. And second, an incredibly straightforward, jargon-free approach to a topic your boss keeps talking about. Be sure to show her the manifesto on page 59, which is worth the entire cost of the book.

Personally, I doubt whether anyone needs an association to dream up new ways to amplify word of mouth. What it does need, and what Andy's busy arguing for, is a group of people who keep pushing each other to do more and more remarkable stuff, to not settle, to create things that are actually worth talking about.

Have fun. Spread the word.

Seth Godin
Author, *Unleashing the Ideavirus*

Preface

This is a book for everyone who has something to sell.

Word of mouth marketing isn't just for multinational corporations with huge marketing budgets. The ideas and practical information you'll find here will work just as well for a dry cleaner, a restaurant owner, or a dentist as they will for a Fortune 500 company. You don't need to be a marketing genius or an I-only-wear-black advertising guy.

Why? Because word of mouth marketing isn't about marketers or marketing. It's about real people and why those real people would want to talk about you and your stuff.

From here on out, I'll use the term *stuff* for *products and services*. Word of mouth marketing works for any kind of product or service. It also works for causes, ideas, charities, and organizations—anything that you want people to talk about.

I've been marketing for a long time, but I've never had a marketing budget. Despite that, I've sold a lot of stuff. Any success I've had has always been half creativity and half talking to a lot of people. I didn't know it at the time, but it was always about what we now call *word of mouth marketing*—joining in the conversation that consumers are having every day with other consumers.

In 2004, I helped start the Word of Mouth Marketing Association, a trade association where all these amazingly smart marketers are evolving word of mouth marketing from a back-of-the-envelope casual practice into a real marketing profession. It's given me the opportunity to work side by side with some of the most brilliant marketers in the world, learning from them and innovating with them. The lion's share of the ideas here are shamelessly theirs, and I owe a deep debt of gratitude. You're getting the inside scoop, right from the source, condensed and highlighted.

Good Marketing Is Easy

One of the most important things I've learned is that word of mouth marketing can be so easy and obvious that everyone misses just how easy and obvious it is. I get dozens of calls and emails every day from people asking how to get started. Small companies, big companies, everyone. There are a number of great books on the topic, but they are often high level or theoretical. It seems there isn't a simple how-to-get-started-with-word-of-mouth book.

So here you go.

This book is full of inexpensive things that you can do today to get word of mouth started. There are tons of ideas here. You can start with steps as basic as a clever product name, a special service, a choice of uniform, a well-worded email, or being a little bit nicer to your customers.

People often say that I make marketing seem too simple. I disagree. Marketing shouldn't be hard, and the best marketing never is.

This isn't a book about advanced techniques. You're not going to find any advice here that asks you to hire an agency or spend a lot of money. I will mention some of the expensive-but-effective tactics just so you know what they are. Many amazing agencies are out there that can help you create amazing word of mouth, and I recommend you talk to them.

But this is a do-it-yourself book. This is what *you* can do to get people talking about your company.

You'll it do well.

A Promise

When you are done with this book, you will be able to try one or two of the techniques I've talked about the next day, without spending more than $50 or a few hours of your time. The day after that, you'll have more people talking about your company. A week later, you'll have a lot more. Then you can dig in and really do it big.

Introduction

People love to talk.

People talk about products and services. People talk about hair color, cars, computers, sandwiches, TV shows, and floor cleaner. The stuff they use every day.

People are talking about you and what you sell right now.

It might be a casual mention. It might be a scathing attack. It might be a scathing attack posted to Amazon, where 20 million people will read it before deciding whether or not to buy your stuff.

Or—it might be something really nice.

How much they love what you do. How their friends just have to try it. Why you are definitely better than the other guys. How wonderful it is to do business with you.

Maybe they'll say these nice things to their neighbors, or write them on a blog, or review you on Amazon, where 20 million people will read it and decide to buy your stuff. This is, of course, what you'd like to have happen. And it's actually pretty easy to do.

Word of mouth marketing is about earning that good conversation.

It doesn't matter whether you're selling real estate, jelly, or jet engines. People will ask other people about you before they decide to buy from you. We turn to people we trust first—friends, family, coworkers, and other people like us—when starting to look for something to buy. Not ads, not brochures, not phone books.

So, what is word of mouth marketing? In this book, I define it as "Giving people a reason to talk about your stuff, and making it easier for that conversation to take place."

In the end, marketing is pretty easy: If people like your stuff, and if they trust you, they will tell their friends to do business with you.

Learn to make customers really, really happy. It doesn't take much more than that.

Understand this concept, devote yourself to it, and you will be a successful word of mouth marketer.

It's More Than Just Marketing

This is nominally a book about a specific marketing technique. But it's really a new philosophy of business (and how to live it).

It's about honesty and admiration. It's about making people happy.

It's a simple philosophy, a new golden rule:

> **Earn the respect and recommendation of your customers, and they will do the rest.**
>
> ■ **Treat people well; they will do your marketing for you, for free.**
> ■ **Be interesting, or be invisible.**

When people trust you, they are willing to put their words on the line for you. Please them, inspire them, and they'll bring their friends to you.

What are your other options? Bore them—and be forced to spend millions in advertising to get them interested. Annoy them—and watch your customers walk away, taking their friends with them.

Advertising is the price of being boring. If your customers won't talk about your stuff, you have to pay newspapers and TV shows to let you do it yourself. That's why you see lots of ads for cereal and toothpaste.

Word of mouth marketing is more than just marketing. It's about making your stuff and your company worth talking about.

How can you become buzzworthy?

Leveling the Playing Field

Word of mouth marketing works for any size business. You don't need to have a hot website, to be in a sexy industry, or to have a cool, innovative new technology. You can make it work if you're the one person who gets it inside a giant corporation. You can make it work for a single store with no advertising budget.

You just have to give people something to talk about.

I love Mario's Barbershop in Chicago. When I go in with my two-year-old son, they offer me a cocktail. They offer him a toy car. It's a guy place. No one ever accepts their drinks, but it's a blast to hang out with Mario, Zoran, and Bobby.

Those drinks are a reason to talk. I tell the other dads at day care. It comes up at parties. It's the first thing that comes to mind when someone mentions a haircut.

The result: A line of dads and toddlers out the door every Saturday. (A Supercuts on the same block is deserted.)

When I was single, there was no better date restaurant than Otello's in Washington, D.C. When I showed up with a woman, the owner would come out before the meal with a big, "It is soooo good to see you again. We are soooo happy you are here." (Of course, he had no idea who I was.) After dinner, he'd produce two glasses of cheap wine, on the house. This guy knew how to make sure you looked like a high roller.

You can only guess how many word of mouth recommendations he got.

There are hundreds of examples just like this of simple ways to get people talking (most don't involve liquor).

Seth Godin calls it being "remarkable" in his book *Purple Cow*. *Remarkable* means worth remarking on, worth saying something about. It's the root concept of word of mouth marketing.

It's Not About the Internet and Blogs

One of the great misconceptions about word of mouth marketing is that it's all happening online. The role of the internet and the new ways people use it to communicate are indisputably critical components of the sudden spread of word of mouth. Blogs are a big deal because they empower lots of people to share ideas.

But that's only a part of it—only about 20 percent of word of mouth happens online. When it does play a role, it usually sparks the 80 percent of word of mouth conversations that actually happen face to face.

So, let me apologize up front. A lot of the examples here are about things you can do with the internet. These stories tend to make good examples. I talk about blogs and online communities because the word of mouth you find there is very visible—it's written down publicly for everyone to see. Many of the recommendations you'll read involve things you can do online, because it's the easiest way to reach people. But word of mouth is not just about the internet and not just for online businesses.

Real word of mouth dips in and out of different spaces. You eat at a good restaurant. You mention it to people at the office. One of them emails your recommendation to his wife. She emails four friends, and they have lunch there. Two mention the restaurant to other friends at a party, and one of them blogs it. Someone reads the blog and calls a buddy about eating there. You get the idea.

Word of Mouth Marketing Makes Us More Honest

Now, here's where it gets interesting. Word of mouth marketing only works if you have good products and services. It only works if people like you and trust you. (If you're a jerk, word of mouth will backfire horribly on you.)

If your product or service sucks, no PR campaign, clever TV ad, or announcement on your website will make consumers believe that it doesn't. Not anymore. And the speed of word of mouth on the internet spreads the truth almost instantly.

You don't hear a lot of good word of mouth about cable companies.

When word of mouth works, good companies are rewarded with gobs of free advertising and attention, and they make more money.

When word of mouth works *better,* bad products and bad companies are punished with negative buzz, and they lose customers.

Think about what this means for you and your family. We have a new social force that rewards companies with free marketing, sales, and profits when they treat people well and produce good products. The same force stops companies from treating people badly, by killing their sales.

For the first time in the history of modern business, we have a *force for good* that is also driven by the *all-powerful profit motive.* For years, government regulators and consumer advocates have tried to use legal and public pressure to make companies treat people well. I'll bet that the profit motive works better.

This is why word of mouth marketing is so exciting. Everyone can do it. It makes money. It makes products and services more exciting. It makes business more honest and ethical.

It's better for all of us.

Everyone Is Already Talking About You

So here's the deal: You're getting talked about whether you like it or not. The conversation has started, so you might as well get involved.

A lot of that talk is happening online. Research from Pew Internet reports that 32 million people are posting content to message boards, and Technorati reports that 13 million people blog weekly.

But even more is happening offline—as it always has. Each and every one of us talks to a friend or family member before we buy something. We listen to our friends before we bother going to a store or restaurant. And we don't just ask for advice—we all make recommendations, too, about what we liked and what we hated.

Yes, it's uncomfortable. The first time you search the blogs for your product name, it's usually a real surprise. Sort of like walking into a crowded party, when the laughter suddenly stops and everyone looks at you.

But it's different. Because everyone is waiting for you to join the conversation. The door is open, everyone is listening, and they want you to be a part of it. So jump in.

But what about the negative? What if people say bad things about you?

Too late—if it's going to happen, it's going to happen. Unless you're the perfect company, it probably already has.

So you only have two choices: let people talk about you, spread rumors, and get it wrong; or join in, participate, and make it work for you.

The best part is, the more you participate, the more the conversation grows, and the more it is about you. Feed it, put the good stuff out there, and the conversation will be dynamic and positive. That's what this book is about—learning the right way to participate and make the most of this wonderful opportunity.

THE ESSENTIAL
CONCEPTS

CHAPTER ONE

What Is
Word of Mouth
Marketing?

GET PEOPLE TALKING

Here's the definition of word of mouth marketing:

> **Giving people a reason to talk about your stuff**
> **and**
> **making it easier for that conversation**
> **to take place**

There are fancier definitions that we can use. The Word of Mouth Marketing Association defines word of mouth marketing as "The art and science of building active, mutually beneficial consumer-to-consumer and consumer-to-marketer communications."

I prefer to keep it simple: It's everything you can do to get people talking.

If you like acronyms, think of it this way:

Word of Mouth is "CtoC" Marketing

You've heard about business-to-business (BtoB) and business-to-consumer (BtoC) marketing. Word of mouth marketing is about real people talking to each other—consumer to consumer (CtoC)—instead of marketers doing the talking.

Actually, it's BtoCtoC. Your job as a marketer is to put out an idea worth talking about. That's marketing. When a real person repeats it, that's word of mouth. It's about the second hop (and the third hop, and the fourth hop, and so on).

Right after our son was born, my wife and I saw an ad for a weekly show at our local movie theater where you were encouraged to bring infants. Now featuring screaming and pooping right in the theater! What a great idea! Any parent of a newborn knows that you're probably not going to see another movie together until the kid gets old enough to be embarrassed to be seen with you.

What was the first thing we did? We called every other parent in our apartment building and brought them with us. The promotion that we saw was traditional marketing. The 12 conversations we had with other parents was word of mouth marketing at its best.

It's All About the Second *M*

Word of mouth has been with us forever. What's new is the second *M*—marketing.

Word of mouth exists. Word of mouth *marketing* is learning to work with it toward a marketing objective.

Word of mouth *marketing* is a new specialty that is as action-able, trackable, and plannable as any other form of marketing.

Word of mouth is natural conversation between real people. Word of mouth *marketing* is learning to work within this conversation so people are talking about you.

Word of mouth is about genuine consumer conversations. Word of mouth *marketing* is joining that conversation, partici-pating in it—but never, ever manipulating, faking, or degrading its fundamental honesty in any way.

Why Now?

If word of mouth has been around forever, there must be some reason why marketers suddenly began talking about it.

Here's what's new: We can finally do something about it.

It's evolved from *anecdotal* to *actionable,* from something that just happens to something you can influence. Word of mouth marketing has become the fastest growing form of marketing because we now have the tools and knowledge to work with it.

Up until a few years ago, we sort of wished that good word of mouth would just happen on its own. You could have a special sale or do some silly publicity stunt and hope people would talk.

Now we can work with people who want to talk about us and help their ideas reach a new audience. We can provide a plat-form so more people hear what our fans are saying. We can use the internet to give far more visibility to a conversation that has always been happening.

We've also gained the ability to track and measure that con-versation. Thanks in part to blogs and the web, we can see who is saying what about us. We can listen to the conversation and understand it. We can figure out who is talking and why they are talking. It's not such a mystery anymore.

Family legend tells that my grandfather Gene was the first person to hire a teenage Elvis Presley to perform in public. He had this unknown kid play his guitar from the back of a truck in the parking lot of the department store where he worked in Memphis. I'm sure it got some people talking, but it wasn't a big deal at the time.

These days, we'd do it a little differently. We'd announce the concert on the web. We'd email a note to people who blog about the local music scene. We'd give flyers to kids at local high schools and invite them to a free show. We'd put the invitation in an email so it could get easily forwarded. We'd try to hire a band with a big following on MySpace, so it could get its fans to show up. We'd use all those cheap and easy things that get lots of people talking.

Later, I'll go into detail on these techniques and explain how to make them work for you.

It's More Than Marketing (or Maybe Not Marketing at All)

In many cases, word of mouth marketing isn't actually "marketing" at all. It's about great customer service that makes people want to tell their friends about you. It's about fantastic products that people can't resist showing to everyone.

This is called *organic* word of mouth—word of mouth that springs naturally from the positive qualities of your company. Many experts would argue that this is the only legitimate form of word of mouth. The opposite concept is *amplified* word of mouth—word of mouth that is started by an intentional campaign to get people talking. I like the organic kind better, but I'll talk about both.

I like the idea that consumers reward companies that have earned their respect with great word of mouth. Nothing beats coming up with a product so interesting that people just can't help talking about it. Nothing is better than customers taking it upon themselves to support a business that they just love.

TiVo is the classic example. They aren't known for their advertising. In fact, TiVo has hardly advertised at all. But everyone knows what TiVo is.

TiVo owners are maniacs. They absolutely will not stop talking about their TiVos. They will chase you down and drag you to their living room to make you see a demonstration. Their love for the product turns them into crazy, passionate, word of mouth promoters.

You see the same passion from people who love OXO utensils, Aeron chairs, or Camper shoes. You see it from Yankees fans and teenagers in love with rock bands.

Organic word of mouth is created by products that get your customers to love you so much that they just can't shut up.

And sometimes the best word of mouth is exceptional customer service—think of the famously generous return policies of Nordstrom or the fact that Enterprise Rent-A-Car will pick you up at home.

I pay a little more than I should to do business with my cell phone company and my web-hosting company, because they answer my calls on the first ring and they usually solve my problems on the first call. Of course, I also tell everyone who asks that they'd be crazy to work with anyone else.

There's a great little conference call service in Fairfield, Iowa, called Conference Calls Unlimited. Pretty much all conference call services look the same and do the same thing, so it's difficult to stand out from the crowd. It's a boring business, and advertising is expensive and ineffective when you sell the same thing as everyone else.

So what did they do? They stopped advertising. They put everything they had into customer service.

These guys will do anything for you. They take care of their customers, whatever it takes. It's surprisingly pleasant and interesting to work with them, despite the uninteresting nature of what they sell.

As you can imagine, the word of mouth they get is fantastic. This isn't the first book to mention this tiny company.

Traditional marketing is no longer the safe way to go. It may make you more comfortable, but it is becoming gradually less and less effective for more and more companies. It's time to focus on making customers happy—earning their trust and respect and getting them talking about your stuff.

THE FOUR RULES OF
WORD OF MOUTH MARKETING

Rule #1: Be Interesting

Nobody talks about boring companies, boring products, or boring ads. If you want people to talk about you, you've got to do something special. Anything. If you are boring, you'll never get a moment of conversation. Your word of mouth will fall flat on its face. (Actually, it will just fade away, unnoticed.)

Before you run an ad, before you launch a product, before you put something new on the menu, ask your spouse about it. Trust me—if he or she finds it interesting, you've got a winner.

Take a trick from the Chicago Bagel Authority's 56 bizarrely named sandwiches, like the Hoosier Daddy and the Muenster Mash. Or the seven-inch-high corned beef sandwiches at New York's famous Carnegie Deli. It would still be the best corned beef sandwich in the world if it were a normal size. But its insane mass guarantees that hundreds of tourists leave there every day to spread the word about one of the greatest sights in the Big Apple.

There are probably hundreds of shoeshine stands in New York City. But everybody goes to Eddie's in Grand Central station. And they tell their friends to make a special trip to go there (passing plenty of other good shoeshine stands on the way). Why? Eddie's has huge, comfy, old-school, red leather easy chairs to sit in. You feel like a king when you sit back and enjoy a few minutes of peace in those chairs at the end of the day.

Give people a reason to talk about you.

And please, I beg you, stop for a minute before you buy more advertising. Think about how much money you are about to spend. Think about how fast you, and everyone else in the world, flip past hundreds of ads without even noticing them.

Don't run another ad unless it is truly worth talking about.

Rule #2: Make People Happy

Happy customers are your greatest advertisers.

Thrill them.

Create amazing products. Provide excellent service. Go the extra mile. Make the experience remarkable. Fix problems. Make sure the work you do gets people energized, excited, and eager to tell a friend.

When people like you, they share you with their friends. They want to help you, they want to support your business, and they want their friends to enjoy what you offer. You will get more word of mouth from making people happy than anything else you could possibly do.

You can make people happy by producing really great stuff—products that do what they are supposed to, that are a pleasure to use. You can also make people happy by treating them well, by providing great service.

Let's look at one of the great mysteries of the modern age. In 1999, why did 60,000 people drive their plain Saturn sedans to Spring Hill, Tennessee, to meet the people who made them? What car could possibly be less interesting than a Saturn?

The annual Saturn Homecoming was a great word of mouth marketing strategy. But it wouldn't have worked if people didn't trust and respect Saturn. People really liked the company. They liked its attitude. They felt taken care of by the nice salespeople and the company's no-haggle concept. They were amazed when they got a friendly note twice a year with instructions on how to adjust their car's clock for daylight savings time.

So they told their friends. They went the extra mile. They supported the company that supported them.

Let's look at another great mystery of the modern age. Why do some people like Target so much? This I won't attempt to explain, but I'm not the only guy who, while on vacation, has been taken to visit a Target *that looks exactly like the one we have at home.* (Aargh.) But they have some stylish stuff. Decent prices. Clean stores. A fun attitude.

Target makes my wife happy in a way that would threaten a less manly man.

And she talks to everyone about it.

Rule #3: Earn Trust and Respect

If you don't have respect, you don't get good word of mouth.

Nobody talks positively about a company that they don't trust or like. Nobody puts their name on the line for a company that will embarrass them in front of their friends.

Always be an honorable company. Make ethics part of everything you do. Be good to your customers. Talk to them. Fulfill their needs.

Make people proud to tell your story to everyone they know.

Southwest Airlines is one of the most trusted brands in the world. It treats its customers well, with few hassles and a great attitude. It treats its employees well, with stable jobs, a no-layoff policy, and decent pay. People like Southwest. People like the company so much that they sent cash to the airline after 9/11 to help it out.

Lots of people are spreading great word of mouth about Southwest. Does anyone have anything good to say about most other airlines?

Every company can be nicer, and every employee can work to make his or her company a little better to its customers.

My bank, Washington Mutual, offers pretty much the same services as every other bank. But they are really nice. Really, really nice. They remember my name and my wife's name. They even remember my two-year-old's name, and he doesn't do much banking. I banked at one of the top three banks for ten years, and at one time my company had more than $1 million on deposit. I could barely get them to cash a check or take my calls. And, after a while, the random, punitive fees started to eat away any respect I had for this venerable institution. Negative word of mouth from people like me has sent a whole lot of money to banks that treat people better.

Rule #4: Make It Easy

Word of mouth is lazy. You've got to help it along if you expect it to go anywhere.

You need to do two things: Find a super-simple message, and help people share it.

Start with a topic that anyone can remember. Something like, "Our software doesn't crash," or, "They have chocolate cream cheese!" or, "They give you snacks while you're waiting for a table," or, "Stupid name, but it sure does work." (Anything longer than a sentence is too much. It'll get forgotten or mangled.)

We all think of Steve Jobs as the greatest computer marketer who ever lived. So what did he do when he returned to Apple in 1996 with the mission of reviving a stumbling company? Did he talk about great software? Stable operating systems? No.

Jobs's great marketing insight was . . . pink and purple computers.

It got everyone talking. It restarted positive word of mouth about the company. Everyone told a friend, because they had a simple topic of conversation that was interesting to share. And when people heard about the cute computers, they were ready to take another look at the more important features.

Once you've got your big word of mouth idea, find a bunch of ways to make it easier to spread. There are countless easy ways to make your ideas portable. A special announcement on a website or brochure is stuck in place. Put it in an email, though, and it's in motion.

THE THREE REASONS
PEOPLE TALK ABOUT YOU

You won't get good at word of mouth marketing until you really understand what motivates people to talk about the stuff they talk about.

People love to talk and share opinions. They love to talk about other people and ideas, and they love to talk about stuff to buy, from the sexy and fun to the dull and mundane.

Three basic motivations drive word of mouth conversations.

The Three Reasons People Talk About You

The Stuff	Feeling Good	Feeling Connected
It's about *YOU:* The marketer and products	It's about *ME:* The talker	It's about *US:* The group of enthusiasts
• They love you (and your stuff). • They hate you. • You've given them something to talk about. • You've made it easy for them to talk about you.	• They feel smart. • They feel important. • They want to help people. • They want to express themselves.	• They are part of the brand family. • They are part of a team. • They are insiders.

Reason #1: They Like You and Your Stuff

People talk because you're doing or selling something that they want to talk about. They love your products. They like how you treat them. You've done something interesting.

It's about giving them a reason to talk about you. The more interesting you get, the more motivated the talkers are. Your customers aren't going to love or hate you (or feel indifferent to you) for no reason.

Bottom line: You've got to arouse some passion before your advocates will begin talking about your company. If you've given them something to love, you can build on that. If you've given them something to hate or ignore, you'll have to address that before you can worry about the rest.

A decent product gets recommended to a friend, but only passively—usually when they are asked directly about it:

"What kind of grill should I buy?"

"I've got a Weber; it's pretty good."

You get much more word of mouth when you make your products cool. The more you make your product buzzworthy, the more it pushes itself into the conversation. The special satisfaction that people get from something great is what moves them from being a passive recommender to an active one:

"Check this out. My new grill has a Pork-A-Licious Thingama-bob. You've got to try it!"

What makes your product worth talking about?

Now, being worth talking about doesn't mean being complicated or expensive.

Let's look at a $2 pen, the Zebra F-301. I mean, what is there to talk about, really? A pen is a pen. It has ink, and it writes. What's the big deal?

Well, it turns out that it's a pretty good pen. No radical leap forward in pen technology, just a cool-looking, stainless-steel, smooth-writing pen that people want to talk about. It's so good that it has inspired actual fans, and a huge amount of word of mouth. Fans who write hundreds of product reviews and blog posts raving about . . . a $2 pen.

Giving people something to talk about also means being creative with how you present your products, services, and company. The day-to-day existence of your business doesn't provide a reason to talk. You've got to keep putting new topics out there.

Even your most die-hard fans need something new to keep them interested on an ongoing basis. Without that extra oomph, you don't have a conversation. But when you do something special, your fans go bonkers.

We all love White Castle (in that Rolaids kind of way). And White Castle gets decent word of mouth. People talk about it, even make movies about it. But it's not a part of day-to-day conversation. So what did White Castle do? It announced that you could make reservations at White Castle on Valentine's Day. What a silly idea. What a wacky dinner date. What a great reason to talk.

You don't need to be that clever. You just need to keep it fresh. If nothing special is happening at your business, there is no reason for anyone to talk about you. Find something. Do a promotion, publish a report, have a sale, stock a new line of products. Anything.

Reason #2: Talking Makes Them Feel Good

Word of mouth often comes down to emotion more than products or product features. We're driven to share by feelings that are far more about us as individuals than about what a business is doing.

The emotions that drive us to talk aren't complicated.

We Want to Look Smart. A lot of people get their kicks out of being the expert on their favorite subject. When we tell people about what to buy, we're showing off what we know. Some people do this really well, and everyone goes to them for advice. Melanie, the scrapbook guru. Bob, the HVAC king. Steve, the car guy. We love to ask these people for advice when we're making a purchase, and they love to show what they know.

With blogs and online communities, it's gone to a whole new level. People put up pages where they share what they know. It becomes a labor of love. They are out there as the expert in the eyes of everyone. You also see these people on message boards, those die-hard volunteers who answer everyone else's questions.

We Want to Help Other People. The desire to look smart is often paired with a higher-level motivation, to help other people. Some people are so passionate about what they know that they want everyone else to enjoy what they are enjoying. It kills them to see someone buy the wrong brand or get stuck with an inferior product.

These are the folks who come up to you in a store when you're trying to decide what to buy and give you an unprompted sales pitch for what they think is the greatest product in the world. Annoying, yes, but driven by a genuine desire to help you out.

Ever met a Macintosh groupie? How could you not? A certain kind of Mac user is so emotionally connected to the brand that they want everyone else to use it. They believe it will surely make everyone's life easier . . . and possibly cause peace on earth.

We Want to Feel Important. Some people talk because they like being asked. They get a kick out of being the expert. The more people ask for their advice, the more important they feel. It feels good to be an authority figure.

Find ways to recognize those customers and give them higher status simply by acknowledging them, keeping them in the loop, and asking for their input. Being a frequent flyer used to be as much about the gold luggage tag as the miles and rewards.

These customers will talk about you and your stuff because it shows off their importance and expertise and because they feel like they're in the inner circle.

We Want to Express Ourselves. Like it or not, the brands that we choose tell people a lot about ourselves. When we talk about a store, or music, or products, it's a way to show off who we are. I'm consistently amazed that the most rebellious teenager, who would drop dead if you called her a "conformist," will proudly wear the logo of Gap or Abercrombie & Fitch. The opposite case has the same effect, when we wear an obscure brand or T-shirt solely for the appreciation of someone like us who might get it, too.

One of the quickest and easiest ways to express our personality and individuality is to talk about the products and brands that we like. Our jeans, our cars, where we shop, and the beer we drink all are ways we show who we are.

It happens a lot among people who don't know each other very well; but even with our close friends, we share information about products and services all the time. Talking about products is our way of helping turn people on to something cool or impressing them by showing them we're hip to something no one else has heard of yet.

Reason #3: They Feel Connected to the Group

The desire to be a part of a group is one of the most powerful human emotions. We want to be connected, very badly.

Talking about products is one way we achieve that connection.

We are emotionally rewarded when we share excitement with a group that has a common interest. We share a bond with people who like the same teams or bands that we do, and we feel a similar connection with those who like the same cars or clothes. The passion generated by being in a group of enthusiasts translates very easily into word of mouth.

Similar phenomena grow around political causes and nonprofit organizations. People can become astonishingly powerful advocates for an issue with which they often have no formal connection. It's interesting to see people who are active volunteers for a cause (such as fighting a disease) that they are not personally affected by. There are a lot of issues to choose from, but being part of a group, any group at all, kicks conversation up to the next level.

Working with this motivation is all about group recognition. It's giving away T-shirts, hats, bumper stickers, or temporary tattoos. It's holding events and rallies that bring people together.

Members of groups that coalesce around specific brands, such as Harley-Davidson riders, Macintosh users, and Nikon owners, are the most likely to talk about the companies' products.

You've got to make these people feel special, feel like part of the family, as though they have some skin in the game.

What About Prizes and Rewards?

Mixing love and money is usually a bad idea.

Offering customers incentives to spread the word about your stuff is often a mistake, and here's why: You make them feel dirty if they're paid for it. Some things just shouldn't be for sale—friendship, certain kinds of favors, and your recommendation.

People are engaging in word of mouth for the reasons mentioned—none of which are about getting paid to do it. When you link a monetary reward (or points or miles) to referring your stuff, you taint the person's motivation for talking about it. It's a kind of bribe. Instead of being a friend recommending a cool product, the person becomes a spokesperson for the company.

Now, to be clear, I'm not saying that incentives or rewards are unethical. I'm saying that they are usually a bad idea that may actually reduce your word of mouth.

The very powerful emotions that create word of mouth, and the resulting affinity with your brand, are nothing to be trifled with. You can deeply insult a loyal talker by offering to pay them for doing it.

Like everything in word of mouth marketing, these ideas are plenty obvious when you think about them. But you'll soon realize that these obvious ideas turn out to be the opposite of what traditional marketing teaches us to do.

A lot of companies offer their current customers rewards for signing up their friends. Whenever I get one of these emails or cards from a friend, I always think, "Well, that's great. You get $50. But what's in it for me?" It turns the friend-to-friend relationship into a salesperson-to-prospect transaction. Even good friends or family members are less believable when they're working for rewards.

But do you remember the original MCI Friends and Family promotion? It was all about mutual benefit. When you told a friend about the program, each of you got a reduced phone bill. You both benefited, equally and together. It kept the motives pure, it respected altruism, and everyone felt good about it. It was all about sharing the savings, not one person making money off the other. It's still one of the greatest word of mouth programs in history.

How to Stop the Word of Mouth Conversation

When you understand why people talk, one more lesson is clear: Overexposure kills word of mouth.

When everyone knows about something, no one needs to talk about it. Nothing could be dorkier than saying, "Hey, have you heard about *The Da Vinci Code?*"

There's an obvious but often overlooked aspect to word of mouth—it is inspired and kept going by newness. When inline skates and Sony Walkmans were new, they were on everyone's lips. Twenty years later, they're not so remarkable.

Krispy Kreme was built on word of mouth. Then they killed the conversation with overexposure.

Remember when those were the most special doughnuts on planet Earth? Krispy Kreme had an amazing word of mouth topic—hot, gooey doughnuts. And a big neon sign that lit up—"HOT NOW"—when fresh doughnuts were coming off the line.

If you lived in a town with a Krispy Kreme, it was an event, even a tourist destination. You did silly things to show it off. When my wife visited a college friend in Toledo, they went on a mission to get those doughnuts at the instant of freshness. There were two stores about a mile apart. They actually drove back and forth between the stores until the light came on and they could dash in to get those hot doughnuts.

Everyone, and I mean everyone, was talking about those doughnuts. The word of mouth gods smiled upon them and their sugary goodness.

Then the company tried to make Krispy Kreme as common as Dunkin' Donuts. What built the chain's great word of mouth—the fact that the doughnuts were hard to get, fresh, and in limited supply—disappeared when Krispy Kreme put its pastries, cold and stiff, on every store shelf. This sudden and massive overexposure killed what was special—in other words, what was buzzworthy or remarkable—about Krispy Kreme.

Nobody tells their friends about food you can buy in a gas station.

THE FIVE Ts OF
WORD OF MOUTH MARKETING

Sometimes great word of mouth is an accident. Sometimes it's a well-planned campaign. Either way, there are certain basic elements that need to be in place for word of mouth to spread like crazy.

They are the Five Ts: Talkers, Topics, Tools, Taking Part, and Tracking.

- *Talkers:* Who will tell their friends about you?
- *Topics:* What will they talk about?
- *Tools:* How can you help the message travel?
- *Taking Part:* When should you join the conversation?
- *Tracking:* What are people saying about you?

I've studied hundreds of great word of mouth successes. Every single one has the Five Ts. It doesn't matter if it's for a big business or a small business, for a Silicon Valley wonder or business-to-business industrial machinery, for a national chain or a single restaurant.

Each time you start a word of mouth campaign, take a few minutes to go through these five steps and figure out how they fit into what you're selling. The process is simpler than you think, and it will guarantee that you'll create effective word of mouth marketing.

#1. Talkers—Find People Who Will Talk About You

Talkers are any group of people who have the enthusiasm and connections to relay your message. Sometimes they are called "influencers" or "evangelists"—but don't let these terms make it sound as though you need some exotic system to find them.

Talkers are regular people. Talkers are your customers, your doctor, your neighbors, your friends.

Sometimes they are new customers bubbling with enthusiasm; sometimes they are rabid fans who volunteer to spread your message. They may be part of a formal word of mouth program, or they may be bloggers who happen to cover your topic.

We all know some talkers. There's the neighbor everyone goes to for advice on travel, the friend who knows every doctor in town, and the coworker who always knows about the best happy hour. Every product has some talkers—and you're probably the talker for something. (What do people ask you about?)

Talkers talk because they love to share great ideas and help their friends. They'll talk about you if you give them something to talk about and if they like you. It doesn't take much more than that.

Don't confuse talkers with trendsetters, celebrities, or journalists. Bellhops, cabbies, and office computer gurus do far more talking, day after day.

The people who will talk about your stuff are closer than you think. Your best talkers are probably customers you interact with every day who would love to be given the opportunity to do a little more.

Think about the fans of a rock band. They spend hundreds of dollars to support and promote a band they love, and they insist that their friends do the same. They *want* to spread the word and will even pay (through purchases of music, concert tickets, T-shirts, and posters) to do it.

Once you identify the right group of talkers, your next challenge is to give them a topic that they are willing to talk about.

#2. Topics—Give People a Reason to Talk

All word of mouth starts with creating a message that will spread.

It doesn't need to be fancy. A special sale, remarkably good service, a cool new feature, a unique flavor, a funny name, or a nice package may be all it takes. The specifics of the message don't matter.

Good topics are portable, clear ideas that one person can repeat successfully.

Commerce Bank is a very friendly, convenient bank, and their motto is "America's Most Convenient Bank." Sort of generic. But their word of mouth topic? A free change-counting machine in the lobby called the Penny Arcade. Everyone talks about the only bank around that will let anyone (even noncustomers) turn change into bills, when most banks won't do it at all.

JetBlue created an amazing topic with their onboard TVs. Now, these TVs are nothing special. (Trust me, basic cable at 30,000 feet is still infomercials and reruns of *Saved by the Bell*.) But it's an easy idea to share. It's easy to repeat. It reminds people of the airline and starts them thinking about the other positive qualities of the brand. No one will tell a friend about the "low-cost, high-personality service model with an efficient structure and dedication to customers that results in quality service." But they will say, "Hey, JetBlue has TV!"

People share surprisingly simple and stupid things. Take a moment and look at your inbox. What have your friends sent you? Jokes, videos, and coupons.

Once you find a topic that is interesting enough to motivate your talkers, your next challenge is to give them tools to help encourage that conversation.

#3. Tools—Help the Message Spread Faster and Farther

Even the best topics need a little help to spread.

Word of mouth marketers make their biggest impact when they provide the infrastructure to help messages travel. The recent growth of word of mouth as a marketing technique is largely due to the growth of the tools that we have to support conversations that are already happening.

Provide the tools that help your messages move farther and faster. An easy-to-forward email and a tell-a-friend button on the order page of your website are two incredibly powerful (but simple) online examples.

Don't let someone leave your store without something to give to a friend, like a menu or a coupon.

Kiehl's cosmetics stores are famous for their free samples. It's impossible to leave without a pocket full of goodies. And they always give you more than one, so you have something to share with a friend.

If someone's got a desire to talk about you, do everything possible to help them along.

Magazines figured this out a long time ago. Although it looks insane, there is a reason why every magazine has a flurry of subscription postcards falling all over your house. People share magazines, and those cards are the tools that help pass along the subscription offer.

A special sale or unique product (the topic) may be worth talking about, but it has exponential marketing power when you pack it into an easy-to-forward email (the tool). A blog is a tool that enables a company to talk directly with fans, giving them a story to share. Online communities create a home and a focus for otherwise disparate conversations. Formal evangelism programs provide the support and encouragement that keep fans talking.

Once you've created tools to accelerate the word of mouth, your next challenge is to keep that conversation fresh and fast-moving by taking part in it.

#4: Taking Part—Join the Conversation

The idea of taking part gives marketers the heebie-jeebies.

Once you open the door to word of mouth conversations, there is no way to shut it again. When you reach out to real people and encourage them to start talking about your brand, they expect you to participate.

When people are talking about you, answer them. Reply to email messages, accept comments on your blog, participate in the discussion board, answer the phone. Thank bloggers who write about you. If you come across complaints, find out why the conversation is negative and fix it. Be helpful. Be truthful. Be thankful. Be nice.

If you don't join the conversation, it will die out. (Or turn against you if you are seen as aloof.)

Yes, it can be scary, especially at first. You'll get negative feedback, you'll even get crackpots, and you'll need to assign staff to listen to and learn from the conversation. At the same time, however, you'll be earning the respect and recommendation of your customers and building powerful long-term relationships.

Once you are a part of the dialog, your next challenge is to track the conversation and learn what people are saying.

#5: Tracking—Measure and Understand What People Are Saying

Amazing tools have been developed that enable us to understand how word of mouth conversations travel and to follow what consumers are saying about us.

Thanks to the popularity of blogs and online communities, people are now writing down every fleeting thought and publishing them online. ("I ate a sandwich. It was tasty. Do you like sandwiches? Comment on my blog!")

Because they are written down, these consumer-to-consumer conversations are easy to find and to measure—a major knowledge boon for marketers. Monitoring online communication lets you understand what consumers really think about your brand, your marketing, and your products. It provides a level of genuine understanding that is more authentic than the data from traditional research techniques.

Tracking what is being said about you and your company is now a whole lot easier. You can find every comment about you on every blog and message board, moments after they are written. A deep understanding of the word of mouth being spread about you is now at your fingertips, instantly, for free.

Your next challenge is to learn to value this raw consumer feedback and to use it to build a smarter marketing plan and a better company.

Putting It All Together: The Five Ts in Practice

Let's look at a product with great word of mouth: Quick-Books, made by Intuit. Small business accounting is never fun, but Intuit masterfully uses the Five Ts to keep the word of mouth conversation going.

Accountants are usually the first to recommend an accounting product to their customers. But Intuit realized that they had another great group of *Talkers:* small business owners who answer each others' questions about bookkeeping. Plumbers, graphic designers, hair stylists (you know, regular people) were helping their friends with the day-to-day challenges of running a small business by talking about products.

The *Topic* evolved directly from the choice of talkers. People were telling their friends, "You're not alone; there is a community of users who will help you with your bookkeeping questions."

The *Tool* Intuit uses is a website called "QuickBooks Community" (*www.quickbooksgroup.com*). It's a place where users— and future customers—can find people like themselves and talk about bookkeeping. A plumber with his own business can go to the website and join a conversation with people just like him. The website facilitates the conversation among these regular people who can learn from one another's experience and pass along helpful information about the product. What might have been a private conversation between two buddies is now shared publicly, viewable by millions of potential customers.

Intuit *Takes Part* by joining in the newsgroup conversation. All sorts of Intuit employees are encouraged to jump in and answer questions, solve problems, and be part of the community. In a world where most software companies barely answer the phone, this participation earns them incredible respect— and more word of mouth.

Finally, Intuit *Tracks* the word of mouth with detailed record keeping and ongoing surveys. They use the word of mouth discussion to learn what works, where there are problems, how to improve the software, and how to keep customers happy.

WORD OF MOUTH MARKETING ISN'T DECEPTION

Listen closely:

Deception, infiltration, dishonesty, and any attempt to manipulate consumers or the conversation are morally bankrupt practices. Plus, they just don't work in the long run.

Honest marketers do not do this and will not do this. Dishonest marketers will get caught if they try. Sleazy behavior will be exposed by the public, who will turn on anyone who attempts it.

Word of mouth marketing is not what is known as *stealth marketing:* lying to people or shilling (a marketer pretending to be a regular consumer to promote a product). It's not going into chat rooms with fake identities. It's not posting fake positive reviews on websites. It's not sending employees out to bars disguised as eager fans.

Honest marketers oppose all forms of stealth and deception.

Word of mouth marketing is about listening to consumers and giving them a voice. Stealth marketing is tricking people. You don't get good customers by lying to them.

If you're being sneaky or deceptive, you will get busted. Consumers today are incredibly savvy and independent, with the information and resources to catch you in a lie and tell everyone about it. The power of the consumer voice will make dishonest companies pay a steep price.

Word of Mouth Can't Be Faked

Word of mouth marketing can only succeed when people trust each other to talk honestly about what they like and don't like.

You cannot fake word of mouth. It just doesn't work without the trust. You might be able to fool a few people for a little while.

But in the end, people will figure out that you faked it. Then you get embarrassed, you get enemies, and you get lost sales.

Let's say a restaurant posts fake reviews to a website. It will get noticed. No matter how good you are, website operators are great at sniffing out fake reviews. It's their job to keep their reviews clean and credible. If they didn't police them, no one would trust their sites. So they pay attention.

On a bigger scale, if you post the same review to a bunch of blogs or message boards, people will notice. You can try to hide it, you can try to vary the message, you can use a bunch of user names. You'll still get busted. It's too easy to search for and compare similar posts. The more you post, the more people know you are posting. As soon as one blogger gets suspicious, they'll look you up and see that you've been posting all over the place.

Guess what happens? All of that positive word of mouth that you were hoping to create turns negative. The very same audience that you were hoping to reach with your fake posts will feel deceived and lied to. And they will start spreading attacks on your company all over the web. You'll lose far more business than you ever could have hoped to gain.

Just Be Yourself

As a marketer, you can comment online, you can post on message boards, and you can do it a lot. Participation is welcome in the new world of online communications and communities. But you have to do it the right way.

The difference between deception and honest participation is *disclosure*.

You can be an eager participant as long as you do it in your own name, clearly identifying who you are and what you stand for. Also, insist that any relationship between your business and the people who speak for you be clearly disclosed from the beginning, whether they are employees, customers, or volunteers.

Sony was busted a few years ago for sending out actors to pose as tourists, asking people to take pictures of them with a fancy new camera. When consumers found out that the supposed tourists were hired by the company, they got angry. They had been used.

Now, let's show how it should have been done. What if Sony had created an exclusive "Sony VIP Tester" program? Let people who are true camera junkies sign up. Sent them loaner versions of new cameras. Given them a membership card, a hat, and a camera bag. Made them feel very, very important.

I guarantee that these people would have talked to far more people than the actors ever could. And they would have done it with a genuine passion and enthusiasm that no actor could ever fake. These volunteers would have been more credible because they had status. They would have felt like important people selected by Sony because they are so special. They would have been proud of their affiliation and happy to disclose it.

Disclosure is a positive thing when done well. Smart marketers understand that disclosure makes messages more powerful because it makes them more trustworthy. Disclosure gives status to participants in a word of mouth program, giving them credibility.

Disclosure is good. Demand disclosure.

Word of mouth is about genuine communications. Always be honest. It's the right thing to do—and it works better.

Simple Rules for Staying Honest

Being honest is easy to do.

The first thing the Word of Mouth Marketing Association did was to publish a code of ethics. Go to *www.womma.org* and read it, and download some of the other tools the site offers to help you maintain ethical word of mouth marketing programs.

It really comes down to one simple idea: The Honesty ROI. Follow these rules and you'll stay away from trouble:

> *Honesty of Relationship:* **You say who you're representing.**
>
> *Honesty of Opinion:* **You only say what you really believe.**
>
> *Honesty of Identity:* **You never lie about who you are.**

Be sure to check each word of mouth initiative you start against these simple rules. It's also important to share these rules with the consumers who are spreading the word for you. Teach them these rules, and make sure that they share the rules in turn with the people with whom they are talking.

Make sure that your company has an internal review process and that someone is asking the tough questions. Many great brands have been deeply embarrassed when an uninformed marketer hired an iffy agency to do a dirty stealth campaign. Make your values clear.

Just Say No

Sooner or later, you'll be offered an opportunity to do something deceptive under the guise of word of mouth. A marketing firm will suggest some secret postings. A junior staffer will offer to go into the chat rooms and generate some buzz.

Don't do it.

If you do even a little stealth marketing, word will get around. And if consumers catch you doing something just a little sleazy, they are going to assume that you're completely sleazy.

This perception snowballs out of control very quickly. In the early days of the internet, pretty much everyone sent email to people who didn't want it. By the time we figured out how much people hated it, the use of all marketing email was tainted.

There isn't a business out there that didn't contribute a little bit to the spam problem.

What happened? Reporters and consumers started referring to all email from businesses as "spam," lumping in responsible messages from respected brands with the worst kinds of trash. Everyone stopped talking about honest ways to use email. Few companies fought for antispam laws. And the spammers ran free, unopposed.

We must not repeat the unhappy history of email marketing. Your inbox (and your kid's inbox) will never be free of spam, and while email marketing still works, it will always have a reputation problem. We must make sure no one confuses

---

The Rules of Honest
Word of Mouth Marketing

1. Word of mouth isn't stealth.
It's open, honest communications with customers and the community.

2. Fake word of mouth doesn't work.
You will get busted. When you get busted, the backlash will destroy your reputation.

3. Oppose all deception.
Protect the trust in genuine word of mouth—
for yourself as a marketer and for your family as consumers.

4. Follow the Honesty ROI.

word of mouth marketing, which is by its nature about consumer trust, with the worst kind of deception. If that perception sticks, all of your customers will think you're a liar, too.

Draw a line that your company won't cross. Educate your team.

You have to step up now to make sure that your reputation and honest marketing tactics don't get tarred with the actions of a sleazy few.

And when you see a stealth campaign from someone else, step up and say something. Blog it, call a reporter—whatever it takes. Stealth thrives on secrecy, so uncover it.

WORD OF MOUTH HAS ALWAYS
BEEN YOUR BEST MARKETING
(YOU JUST DIDN'T KNOW IT)

Word of mouth has had a far greater impact on your business than you think.

Unfortunately, most businesses do a bad job of measuring it, so they don't always recognize it when they see it. In fact, most marketing reports bury it altogether. The impact of word of mouth is what I call the "hidden statistic."

Problem #1: We Never Call It by Its Real Name

We've just started using the term *word of mouth* in formal marketing. That means that lots of things that should be considered word of mouth are not properly identified as such. This inconsistent naming means that we fail to measure word of mouth accurately.

Take another look at all your sources of new customers. Rename anything that could be considered customer to customer. Give word of mouth its due credit to understand the real impact that it's been having on your business.

Here are some of the hidden names of customer sources that are actually word of mouth:

- From a friend

- From a coworker

- From my boss

- From my doctor

- Online review or article (not an ad that you ran)

- Direct mail sent to someone else at my company

- Cross-reference on Amazon

- Knowing someone who uses it

- Other

- None of the above

- . . . and many more

You probably have a survey, chart, or spreadsheet that reports where your new customers are coming from. It might look something like this:

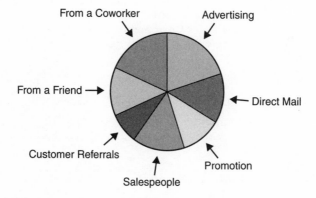

Now, let's rename those sources of customers that are actually from word of mouth:

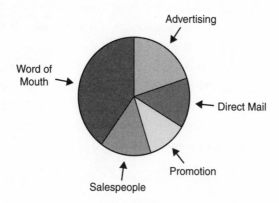

When you reveal those word of mouth sources and name them correctly, it turns out that word of mouth is the most important category.

Problem #2: It's Hard to Divide by Zero

You've probably got another spreadsheet that lays out all of your marketing costs and how much business you got from each of them. It might look something like this:

Source	Cost	New Customers	New Revenue	ROI
Advertising	10,000	12	12,000	120%
Direct Mail	7,000	8	8,000	114%
Promotion	9,000	7	7,000	78%
Sales	15,000	9	9,000	60%

What's missing? Word of mouth!

Why? Because word of mouth usually doesn't cost anything. If we don't have a budget for it and we don't have staff assigned to it, we usually forget to add it to our reports on where our customers are coming from. On top of that, it screws up our spreadsheets, because you can't write a formula to figure the return on a zero-cost word of mouth campaign. So most of us skip it.

Add it in. Take another look, and you'll see something surprising: You're getting far more customers for free through word of mouth than all those other types of marketing.

Remember this: The best value from your marketing investment is the customers you've acquired for free.

The Orphans of Marketing

You've always been doing word of mouth marketing; you just didn't call it that.

Word of mouth marketing is an umbrella term for dozens of different techniques that can be used to energize customers and get them talking. Many of these tactics aren't new, and some are very familiar.

Take another look at some of the specialized marketing tactics that you already know: special sales, loyalty programs, wacky promotions, viral emails, sponsoring a softball team, newsletters, free samples, grassroots political outreach, blogs, partnering with community groups, referral programs, and much more.

These techniques have been used for years by event promoters, small businesses, online marketers, political consultants, loyalty experts, and so on. Now we understand that word of mouth is the thing that ties them all together.

Think about it this way: "Which marketing programs get people talking about me?"

Most of these don't fit into a traditional marketing category like "advertising" or "direct mail" (and you'd have a hard time hiring a traditional agency to do them for you). So they often get neglected or stuck in another department. They are the orphans of marketing.

Many of these orphan techniques actually share a common objective—getting people to talk to each other about you. When we look at them in light of this objective, we now realize that what we now call word of mouth marketing is a unified, plannable marketing practice.

So let's define *word of mouth marketing* as a top-level marketing discipline (like advertising, sales, and PR) and place all of the individual techniques you can use as the tactics within that discipline. Proactively looking at these tactics within the context of word of mouth marketing clarifies the objective and helps you do a better job.

Not only should word of mouth marketing take its place next to other mainstream marketing techniques, it should come first, because it's the cheapest, most effective, and most customer friendly.

Now You Know Just How Important Word of Mouth Is to Your Business

Rescue that orphan.

Put word of mouth at the top of your to-do list. Don't let it get lost, and don't let it get buried under much more comfortable, traditional advertising programs.

Word of mouth marketing has always been your most important source of new business. It's always been your least expensive source of new customers.

It's time for your most effective marketing strategy to become official, to move out of the marketing orphanage. It's time to create a space for word of mouth marketing in your budget and business plan, setting clear objectives and measuring the results.

CHAPTER TWO

Deep Stuff:
Six Big Ideas

CONSUMERS ARE IN CONTROL—
GET USED TO IT

Now you know: People are already talking about you, and they're doing it right now. Will you get involved in what they're saying, or will you let their conversation happen without you?

From here on out, no advertising decision will be made again without a new person at the table: the consumer. No longer do ad agencies, media executives, and reporters control the message. Real consumers, with real communications power, have added their voices to the mix. And their voices are drowning out traditional media. A single consumer voice, in the end, has far more impact than any ad could.

Here's a doozy: Nothing is more powerful than a kid with a blog.

Look at how Google sees it. A customer is looking for information about you. There is only one *New York Times,* and Google only shows a single link to that great article about you that ran last year. (Actually, it usually shows nothing—most of the *Times* articles are password-protected and don't appear in Google at all.) But Google will deliver dozens of blog posts about you, right on top, written by just about anyone. Search engines like blogs, and there are far more blogs than newspapers.

Lots of little consumer-written comments, unedited, get far more exposure than all of the traditional media ever will. Word of mouth drowns out advertising, media, and journalism.

This shift in power from media to consumer can be traced back to a few transformative new realities: mass consumer participation, widespread dissemination of consumer opinion, and the scrambling of old-school media with word of mouth.

The bottom line: Word of mouth is now mass media.

Here's how it happened.

Mass Participation:
We Are Reviewing Like Crazy

From the first time Amazon asked you to write a review, from the first time eBay let you judge a seller, we became a community of armchair critics.

Sharing our opinions has graduated from something small, between friends, to an inextricable part of our culture. Sure, there's always been word of mouth, but it's grown into an active part of our daily lifestyle.

In fact, according to research from Pew Internet, 44 million people have rated a product online. Review site BizRate alone collects more than one million new reviews each month. Every major city has websites that let you review contractors, restaurants, stores, and more. Millions more people are writing their own blogs, joining chat rooms, and reading other people's opinions.

Since Amazon began posting customer reviews on its website in the fall of 1995, dozens of major online retailers, as well as countless specialized product-review sites devoted to sharing consumer opinion, have followed suit, providing a huge, wide-ranging, and permanent record on the word of mouth about almost every product and service imaginable.

But even more is happening offline. And it always has. Each and every one of us talks to a friend or family member before we buy something. We ask our friends before we bother going to a store.

And everyone will say what we think about your business, whether or not anyone asked or cares to listen.

People Like Me

It's more than just the fact that everyone is reviewing everything these days.

We don't rely on the opinions of professional reviewers like we used to. We don't just buy *Consumer Reports* and take its recommendations for what stove to buy; we don't follow Roger Ebert's thumb into the movie theater. Instead, we listen to our friends—the hundreds of thousands of them who post reviews, have their own sites, and constantly tell us what they like and what they can't stand.

Survey after survey, including the Edelman Trust Barometer, finds consumers using the same phrase—*people like me*—when asked whom they turn to. We trust the opinions of people like ourselves more than anyone else. It makes you wonder why companies still pay actors to star in ads, when we'd rather hear from real people.

That trust in real people is being fed by many of the review sites. Amazon highlights reviewers who are willing to post their real name next to their reviews. Other sites let you rate the reviewers, giving you the word of mouth on the word of mouth.

It'd be impossible to meet each one of the people out there posting reviews, but their collective voice—our collective voice—is being heard and followed.

Online stores help this along by giving us the collective opinions of lots of people like us. We don't know everyone who posts online reviews, but we can trust the opinion of a large group. It's hard not to notice 139 negative reviews, just as 400 raves mean that something is probably pretty good. Even if you give the opinion of one expert more weight than any one amateur, you can't dismiss an avalanche of criticism or praise.

And if that weren't enough, almost all of the sites that post customer reviews analyze and summarize the data for us. We know the average number of stars a product gets before we even reach the product description page.

No marketer can ignore the fact that "people like us" are out there, and they are sharing what they feel.

Mass Dissemination:
What We Say Goes Everywhere

We all remember the classic shampoo commercial. Say it with me: "She told two friends, and they told two friends, and so on . . ." Of course, it didn't really work like that. You told two friends, one of them told her sister, and that was about it.

It all changed when we went online, where mass dissemination is guaranteed.

When even a simple email can be picked up by a friend and forwarded to a list of 500 people (who then could forward it to everyone they know, too), word is spreading faster than we could ever hope to control.

Advertisers used to be able to reach 80 percent of buyers with ads on the big three television networks. Now, any old Joe can reach most of your future customers with a few well-placed online reviews. A slight change in the balance of power, to say the least.

It's a marketer's fantasy: You could have a salesperson standing in the aisle next to every one of your products in every Sears store in the world, saying nice things. Of course, this is impossible.

But regular consumers can say those things on the Sears website, right there next to the "Add to Cart" button.

The blogs just spread the word of mouth faster. Anyone can set up a free blog in five minutes. They can type what they want about your business, and it's online for everyone to see. Now just because something is blogged, that doesn't mean anyone is reading it. But one blogger links to it, and she tells two bloggers, and they tell two bloggers . . . You get the idea. Plus, every time a potential customer is researching a purchase, that silly little blog post shows up. It may not be a well-read page, but it's seen when it matters—when someone is ready to buy.

Traditional Media and Word of Mouth Are Forever Intertwined

The professionals used to produce our media for us, but we've lost that clean page of text, written by reporters, edited by editors, and sold in a neat, finished package. We've lost the captive audience watching the pretty ads, displayed on purchased media.

News is now served up á la carte by search engines and bloggers. You don't always see the story as it was originally delivered; instead, you get a link to the middle. You get a random person and her blog connecting what you were looking for to three things you never knew about and then linking to a bigger blogger. The web now inserts rough, raw consumer contributions into web pages, and the search engines grab our messages and show them with an unruly mishmash of homemade thought. And now the bloggers are the mash-up experts, taking all these messages, rearranging, recombining, and rebroadcasting them to massive, willing audiences.

Even a proper newspaper article isn't safe from the consumer voice. Many traditional media outlets now choose to link their stories directly to live blog headlines, breaking down the clean newsroom wall forever. While the official news story sits static on the page, the links next to it are displayed automatically from anyone blogging—without an editor filtering the information. Expect to see this soon in a paper near you.

Picture a hard-working young PR rep who lands a dream story about his client in a high-profile newspaper. He emails his coworkers about it and heads off to the boss's office to share the news. But by the time he gets there and his boss pulls up the web page, the story is already corrupted—the blog headlines sitting next to it are nasty.

Your job: Make sure the word of mouth is good. You can't control the consumer conversation, so remember that PR isn't over when the article is written. The goal is earning good word of mouth on an ongoing basis.

For companies that don't keep their promises, search engines can be even scarier. Let's say that you are spending some big bucks on a search engine marketing campaign. You have nice little ads down the side of the page, all saying, "Click me, we're great." Of course, the bigger links in the middle of the page are from real consumers. You'd better make them happy, or those posts will overpower any paid placement.

Let's look at a certain major cable company we won't name that infuriates its customers again and again with missed service appointments, absurdly poor customer service, and other insulting treatment. When you look this company up online, what do you see? Expensive ads, official news stories—and tens of thousands of posts from angry people. It's good to know that the company can never buy another online ad without having it placed next to the words of a customer they've messed with.

Why is this? How can a single blogger with her list of gripes and raves have more impact than *Time* or *Newsweek*? It's because that person is part of a community—a community that seeks out information about things its members care about and shares those opinions through word of mouth. When one of the members of this community rants against some software that accidentally erased his hard drive, that rant gets picked up by a hundred other sites, each with its own following. Anyone tapped into one of these conversations now has immediate access to the rant—and knows which software company killed someone's computer.

There are a thousand websites for every one traditional newspaper or magazine. There are more independent, individual voices than old media out there today. And because these new voices are easier, quicker, and cheaper to access, they travel farther.

Learn to work in this mixed-up world. Know that people are already talking about you in a conversation that is intense, active, and everywhere.

Marketers who ignore the conversation will be seen as aloof and clueless and will get kicked around. Those who learn how to work with consumers, how to join the conversation, and how to make this work in a positive way will thrive.

Don't hesitate. Get out there and start talking.

UR THE UE

Hey, advertisers! You don't get to tell us what to think about you anymore.

You are not what your ads say or what your brand statement is. You are not what you wish your company to be. You are not the rosy image carefully crafted and projected through a marketing message.

You are the sum total of what people do and feel when interacting with your stuff. You are what real people experience with your company. Write this down:

> **You are the user experience. UR the UE.**

Marketing is what you do, not what you say. The story that will be told by the power of word of mouth is what really happens underneath all the marketing. If you have good products and good services, people will say good things about you. If you fall down on the job, they will say that, too.

With the speed and power of online-assisted word of mouth, you can never hide from this reality. Even a few years ago, you could put out an average product, back it with extraordinary ads, and hope that the feedback wouldn't be heard until enough people had already bought into it. You could put out a bad product and sell it for a long time before people started to realize that it just wasn't any good.

In this new world, you will have product reviews, blog posts, and emails between friends flying around within moments of a new product first hitting the street. You can't push weak products on people when everyone's going to know within 24 hours if they're good or not. Great advertising doesn't fix a car that constantly needs service.

When you are thinking about marketing a new product, what you really should be thinking about is what people will say after they use it—its functionality, its quality, and how you treated them.

Remember the power of the single blogger? She's not going to stand for a shoddy product, and she's certainly not going to stay quiet when that product is backed by flashy ads and false promises. Before you can say "primetime commercial," the blogs and reviews will be full of complaints about the real deal.

A 2006 study by the Verde Group showed that people who hear about a bad shopping experience are less likely than the people who actually had the bad experience to ever set foot in the store. And when you realize that someone who's had an unpleasant encounter with your stuff is going to tell, on average, five other people, you start to see just how damaging bad word of mouth can be in the real world.

Your only choice is to make sure that the experiences people have with your company are positive ones. Make good products. Treat people well. Earn their positive recommendation. Take some of that advertising budget and put it into customer service, because customers' experiences will drive more word of mouth sales than another ad.

Prime examples of this phenomenon are going on right now in the airline industry. As I said earlier, Southwest Airlines gets splendid word of mouth. It offers a fairly nice customer experience in a pretty cruddy industry.

Compare Southwest to Ted, United Airlines' attempt at a word-of-mouth-worthy airline.

We can't fault Ted for trying. It threw every piece of marketing it had at potential customers to convince us that it was special.

But that message isn't actually true. Other than the new coats of paint, most of what the ads claim is special isn't there. Their website goes as far as telling us the services "designed to make your Ted flight both comfortable and memorable" aren't offered on every flight—and you have to pay to get more legroom. Snacks are available, but only on flights longer than two-and-a-half hours and only if you pony up the extra $5.

That Ted couches its shortcomings in a nice-looking website with snappy copy makes it all the more obvious that it subscribes to the "because we said so" marketing technique. Ted wants us to think it's different because it's telling us so. In reality, Ted is the same United with a facelift, unable or unwilling to give its customers anything remarkable.

You can't fake love—or positive word of mouth. The word of mouth will be about the real user experience—how customers are treated at the airport and on the plane. No amount of advertising will change that.

> **Big Idea: Success comes not from what you advertise, but from what you deliver.**

Your customers will keep talking about you if your story matches their experience—good service, no hassles, upheld promises. They'll come back to you because you're you.

The sum of your company isn't what you say your brand is but instead the day-to-day qualities that your products and people express to consumers. What really happens underneath all the marketing is the story that consumer-driven media will tell. No amount of manipulation, obfuscation, inundation, or sheer quantity of advertising will save a bad product or bad company.

If you do what you say, if you choose to be a better business, you will do bigger business.

IT'S ALL ABOUT THE
PERMANENT RECORD

We used to think that the web was a temporary thing. Now we know the truth: Everything lives forever in Google.

The failed ad campaign, the upset customer, the broken product, the post on a message board, the service rep having a bad day. They will never go away.

So you've got a new job to do. Your mission: Make sure that the good stuff gets on the permanent record too. The wonderful product, the staffer who went the extra mile, the problem solved, the complaint answered.

Your real job as a word of mouth marketer is to make sure that the human face of your company gets out there. Participate, rectify, engage, entertain, satisfy, support, and surprise.

Correcting the Permanent Record

Let's face it, we all have stuff we'd prefer to let go. It's not that you'll never make a mistake or draw criticism; it's how you handle it that counts. You'll never be able to control the blogosphere conversation. Don't even try.

But what you can do is participate, earn respect, and tell your story. Jump in, join the conversation, and be a part of it. You can make sure that the conversation ends on a positive note, that your views are heard, and that you're part of the community.

Start thinking about what kind of experiences you are creating for customers and how those experiences are reflected in the record. Evaluate how customer service is handled and how a botched call will ripple through the word of mouth discussion. And compare that to how a little something special will be remembered.

A Better Use of $8 per Hour

Here's a tip: Why not recruit one of your customer service reps (preferably one who can spell) to be a word of mouth service rep? Give a low-level frontline staffer the job of proactively searching the web for any and all word of mouth about your company and your products.

When people are praising your company—thank them.

When people have a complaint, a rant, a slam—fix it.

Every problem festering unsolved is another unhappy customer out there spreading negative word of mouth. Make it right. Every problem is an opportunity to fix the permanent record, to end your story on a positive note.

Everyone makes mistakes. Your mistakes live on, forever, on the internet.

So do the fantastic things you do. Focus on the fantastic.

HONESTY IS THE ESSENCE
OF WORD OF MOUTH

The one truth about word of mouth is that the truth always rises to the surface. The truth about your company, products, services, and people—your stuff—is all that matters now.

You can't hide a bad product behind a great media campaign.

You can't hide bad service behind a big brand.

You can't lie to yourself, and you can't lie to your customers.

Word of mouth and the newly empowered customer voice mean that marketers that sell poor products or don't respect their customers can't get away with it anymore.

Word of Mouth Makes All Marketing More Honest

Word of mouth is the feedback loop that forces marketers to pay attention to the consumer. It brings advertisers out of isolation and forces them to confront the reality of the impact that their products and marketing have on real people. It puts the consumer at the head of the boardroom table.

Word of mouth marketing protects consumers by giving them a voice. This kind of marketing gives a powerful platform to consumers—and makes marketers listen. It empowers consumers by engaging with them online and in the real world. It gives people the power to voice their dissatisfaction and expose dishonesty.

We're the marketers who have learned to listen. Word of mouth marketers don't have a choice. We can't do what we do unless consumers are happily willing to relay our message. So we're getting good at making them happy. Word of mouth is on the rise because marketers have finally begun to understand that a happy customer is the greatest advertisement.

Traditional advertising is hurting because consumers don't trust it, they see through the slick production values, and they tune it out. When consumers trust marketers, they will recommend their products. When all marketers learn to respect consumers' word of mouth, all marketing will be more honest.

We're learning to listen to consumers. We're learning to talk to them. This is a good thing for the future of marketing. All marketers should be held to this higher standard, not only because it's right, but because honest marketing works better.

THE MATH OF CUSTOMER
SATISFACTION

The power of word of mouth fundamentally changes the math of business.

When you factor in the impact of word of mouth, things that look profitable may not be. Ideas that seem smart are often dumb. Unfortunately, not many companies see this because traditional financial reporting doesn't account for word of mouth effects.

Once you understand the math, you'll find that it pays well to treat people well.

One of the big Las Vegas hotels charges $27 per day to use the gym. Hotels are expensive, but that's just insulting. When families get home, what do you think they are telling their friends? "They have a 20,000-gallon fish tank in the lobby?" Probably not. They are saying, "It was nice, but they'll squeeze you for every penny once you get there." This hotel also charges $20 to rent an inner tube at the pool. Good word of mouth isn't spread by parents frustrated because their crying kids didn't understand why Daddy didn't want to get ripped off.

Of course, hotels have done the same thing for years by charging ridiculous amounts for phone calls from the rooms. What's different now is that all hotels are reviewed online. The reviews go up instantaneously, and they never go away. What's different now is that we can talk about these annoying practices with thousands of other people like us. This is exactly the kind of negative word of mouth generator that may make more money in the short term, but hurts your business in the end.

Somewhere there's an accountant with a spreadsheet saying, "Hmmm. Three hundred people a day, 27 bucks a head. That's $8,100 every day, almost $3 million a year in pure profit." The problem is that no one seems to be looking at the other side of the spreadsheet, the side that shows how many custom-ers feel burned by the hotel every day. Traditional cost account-ing doesn't report how many betrayed customers decided never to come back to that hotel or how many friends they shared the story with. I'll bet they've lost far more in loyalty and room rev-enue than they take in at the gym.

One of the most famous word of mouth emails ever is a presentation called "Yours Is a Very Bad Hotel," which was cre-ated by two frustrated businessmen who showed up late one night at a Doubletree and found that their guaranteed room had been sold to someone else. They sat in the lobby and created a scathing, hilarious PowerPoint about the experience. Millions of people have been forwarded a copy of it over the past few years. Doubletree apologized later, but the damage was done.

Three Math Problems

These days, all marketers are obsessed with measuring results, so let's do some math (actually, some story problems).

Problem #1. We just spent $100,000 on search engine advertising. Our ad pops up next to three competitors' ads, alongside the regular search results. But the second and sev-enth results are from the website of an angry customer with the headline "Your Brand Sucks."

What is the cost to our acquisition campaign? How much did we waste? How much business did bad word of mouth drive right to our competitors' ads? How many people clicked on the negative stories?

Problem #2. We spent $5 million to develop and launch a new product. Two grouchy customers post negative reviews on Amazon. More bad reviews follow. In fact, with 125 reviews, the average is 1.5 stars (the lowest rating you can get is 1 star).

Amazon links visitors to competitors' more popular products. One of the same grouchy customers posts negative reviews on three other sites. Customers never show up.

How fast will this product die? How much development investment was lost because we didn't prepare for word of mouth? What are the ripple effects on the rest of our products?

The Worst Reviews Ever

ACT! was once the greatest contact-management software ever. I actually was given version 2.0 by my dad in 1988 (yes, '88), and used it right through 2004. Then they sold me an expensive upgrade that was just awful.

Hundreds of people agreed. Just look at a sample of the some of the headlines from more than 125 negative reviews on Amazon for ACT! 2005:

> Major Step Backwards. Don't waste your money on this product. This product is crap! The worst release I've experienced. Slowest software ever written. Every upgrade ruins my database!!! Punishing Users Daily. Avoid this version. Waste of time. VERY BAD PRODUCT. Don't Do It! ZERO stars. Unusable! Rubbish. Disaster. Stay away!!! . . . and 100 more.

Wow. That's cold.

But the creators of ACT! took their customers for granted, released a bad product—and word of mouth killed them.

Problem #3. We pay for an email campaign to one million opt-in (we hope) email addresses. We get 1 percent click-throughs, and close 10 percent of them, giving us 1,000 new customers. But 10,000 people don't remember opting in. So they get angry and decide never to buy from us again. And they each tell five friends that we spammed them. Two thousand of those people were current clients who are now mad at us. And they each tell five friends.

How many prospects do we lose forever? Was the potential lifetime value of these customers greater than the new accounts we acquired? What is the lost revenue from current customers who left because they think we are spamming? What happens when people start blogging that we spammed them?

A Penny Saved Is a Penny Burned

Let's look at another all-too-common example of bad math: outsourced customer service. (I'm not talking about international outsourcing. Poor telephone service is an equal-opportunity offender that spans race, creed, and nationality.)

Company after company tries to save a buck on low-cost customer service. It doesn't work. When you add in the word of mouth math, you realize that any drop in customer service is a marketing disaster.

It comes down to the concept of "first call resolution"—how many customers were satisfied on their first call. When that number drops even slightly, you've created word of mouth poison.

Think about what happens with every person who gets off the phone with a problem unresolved. They get angry. They tell their friends. The word of mouth starts flying, and it's not pretty. Every day that the problem hangs out there unresolved is another wave of negative word of mouth spreading.

Now, do your math. You saved $5 on a low-end call center rep. But the customer has to call twice, so you're paying twice.

Then, add in those five people the angry customer tells. What did it cost you to get those customers? What will it cost to replace them?

Bad service is expensive. Especially when you look at the marketing cost to replace the leads burned through negative word of mouth.

This Is a Bottom-Line Issue

The trust of the public and the voice of a satisfied consumer are the most powerful assets you have. You need to put those assets in the balance sheet and your business plan. Whether in the fundamental quality of your products, the reliability and courteousness of your service team, or a specific marketing or sales effort, you have to take into account the impact of word of mouth on your bottom line.

WORD OF MOUTH MARKETING
MAKES MORE MONEY

Here's the page that pays for the book. (Show it to your boss.)

Word of mouth marketing is the most profitable marketing you can do. Nothing, I mean nothing, makes you more money. Add these up:

- *Reduced customer acquisition costs.* Word of mouth customers are free. Every one you get lowers your average cost of new business.

- *Free advertising.* Word of mouth promotion doesn't cost a thing.

- *Better return from traditional advertising.* Word of mouth supports your ads' messages and spreads them around.

- *More productive salespeople.* Every salesperson performs better when positive word of mouth is helping them close more deals.

The net impact: More business, higher return on investment, and lower costs. Word of mouth marketing does more than make money on new sales. It makes all of your sales and marketing more effective.

Which leads to another important conclusion: Satisfied customers who will spread word of mouth are the most powerful assets you have.

Protect them.

Treat them with respect.

Listen to them.

You will do better marketing and be a better marketer because of it.

Learn this and you will survive and thrive.

The Word of Mouth
Marketing Manifesto

1. Happy customers are your best advertising.
   Make people happy.

2. Marketing is easy. Earn the respect and recommendation of your customers. They will do your marketing for you, for free.

3. Ethics and good service come first.

4. UR the UE: You are the user experience (not what your ads say you are).

5. Negative word of mouth is an opportunity.
   Listen and learn.

6. People are already talking. Your only option is to join the conversation.

7. Be interesting, or be invisible.

8. If it's not worth talking about, it's not worth doing.

9. Make the story of your company a good one.

10. It is more fun to work at a company that people want to talk about.

11. Use the power of word of mouth to make business treat people better.

12. Honest marketing makes more money.

HOW TO DO IT—
The Five Ts in Action

CREATING A PRACTICAL
WORD OF MOUTH MARKETING PLAN

The first part of this book gave you the background you need to understand the word of mouth phenomenon—why people talk and how businesses should work with word of mouth.

The rest of the book is all about practical steps that you can take to get people talking about you (and help the message spread fast and far). We're going to talk about the hands-on techniques you can use, giving lots of examples that illustrate these techniques in action.

Some of the examples will be things that you can do right away. Some won't apply to your business at all. But everything you read will help give you a feel for the kinds of things you can do to generate word of mouth. When you read the examples and techniques, think about how you would change them to fit your company. There are a dozen ways you could adapt every idea in this book.

Remember, by its nature, each word of mouth moment is original—or no one would be talking about it! Take what you read here as the seeds of ideas, as templates that will help you recognize a word of mouth opportunity when you see it.

So rearrange, rip apart, and rethink everything you read here until it feels like it's right for you. This isn't an instruction manual or a recipe book. There's no specific formula for great word of mouth. Mix and match what you see until you get excited about it. That's when you'll know you've got something that will work.

Finding *Your* Five Ts

To build your plan, you need to walk through the Five Ts and apply each one to your stuff. The following chapters will build out each T in detail. They will explain the most common and most effective techniques and suggest ways that you can use them.

Use the worksheet on the following page as a handy summary and a place to record your plan as it develops. (If you need another copy of the sheet, visit *www.wordofmouthbook.com.*)

Keep It Easy

People will talk about you if you get the basics right.

A few of the techniques I suggest might be complicated or expensive, but most are easy and cheap. As a rule, start with the simple stuff. It usually works great. Complicated word of mouth campaigns work, too, but they may work only for particular businesses or specific industries. If they won't work for you, that's okay.

Here's an easy one if you've got a website: Put a "tell-a-friend" link on every single page. Make it incredibly easy to spread the

The Five Ts of Word of Mouth Marketing

Step	What to Do	Examples	Your Plan
1. Talkers	Find people who will talk about you	Fans, volunteers, customers, bloggers, influencers	_____ _____ _____ _____ _____ _____
2. Topics	Give people a reason to talk	Special offer, great service, cool product, silliness, neat ad, new feature	_____ _____ _____ _____ _____ _____
3. Tools	Help the message spread faster and farther	Tell-a-friend form, viral email, blogs, handouts, samples, message boards, online communities	_____ _____ _____ _____ _____ _____
4. Taking Part	Join the conversation	Let staff surf and reply to comments, post on blogs, join discussions, answer email, offer personal service	_____ _____ _____ _____ _____ _____ _____ _____
5. Tracking	Measure and understand what people are saying	Search blogs, read message boards, listen to feedback, use advanced measurement tools	_____ _____ _____ _____ _____ _____

word when someone feels the urge. Have that link send a cool email that the recipient will want to pass along again.

Here's an easy one if you've got a retail store: Get some great shopping bags. The kind of bag that people will save and use over and over again. Print them with your logo—and some cool, bold design. You'll have a horde of satisfied shoppers walking around, showing you off everywhere they go. People will see the bags, and conversations will start. (Bloomingdale's invented this trick with their "Big Brown Bag." Shoppers like them so much that they actually pay for the bags.) Every shopper becomes a potential word of mouth talker when they have a conversation starter in their hands.

Here's an easy one if you have a restaurant: Give away free food while people are waiting for a table. Every city has a restaurant that does it. Lou Mitchell's in Chicago gives you fresh doughnut holes and Milk Duds. Everybody knows about it, and everybody talks about it. No one is saying, "Hey, you've got to get the turkey sandwich at Lou Mitchell's." But the doughnuts and Duds are the first thing anyone mentions when you ask for a restaurant recommendation in that neighborhood.

Whatever business you're in, ask yourself these questions when you're looking at a customer:

- When she walks out the door, what have I given her to talk about?

- How will he remember to tell his friends?

- Could I have made it easier for her to talk to more people about me?

- Was anything about his experience remarkable?

There are hundreds of other ways to get people talking, but you only need one good one to change your business forever. A silly something, a special moment, service with a smile. Anything worth talking about.

Marketing doesn't get any easier than this.

CHAPTER FOUR

Talkers:
Who Will Tell Their
Friends About You?

All marketing has a medium. An advertisement's medium is
TV, newspapers, radio, or any other place that carries ads.
Direct mail works through the post office.

The medium of word of mouth marketing is real people.

You need to find the right people to carry your message, just
as an advertiser needs to find the right programs and publications. Some people will love to talk about you, some won't care,
and some may want to talk but have nothing nice to say.

YOUR JOB:
FIND THE PEOPLE WHO LIKE
TO TALK ABOUT YOU

One of the reasons word of mouth marketers place so much emphasis on respect and honesty is because of our reliance on the trust of real people. We must protect the human medium just as carefully as editors protect the journalistic integrity of a newspaper. We owe a deep debt to those who help spread our message, and we repay it by treating them well.

A good word of mouth program is built on how you take care of your talkers:

- Identify the right talkers

- Create a communications channel to reach them regularly

- Give them the topics to talk about

- Keep them happy and motivated

To do these things really well, always remember the three reasons people talk. They want to feel good, they want to help others, and they want to belong to a group. Work with these motivations to keep people talking.

WHO ARE THE TALKERS?

Usually your talkers are obvious. They are those happy customers who are eager to share their enthusiasm with their friends. Every business has a core of customers who are active recommenders. Sometimes, talkers are customers who have the outgoing personality to talk about things they like. Or they may be customers who are less proactive but who are the kind of people who often get asked for advice.

But talkers can be much more than just customers. They can be super-eager fans who will never buy a product. Ferrari has many more talkers than customers. They get word of mouth from noncustomers—eager kids, sports car freaks, reporters, and enthusiasts of all sorts.

When Wynn Las Vegas opened its massive, lavish hotel/casino, it turned to the most important talkers in town: cabbies. The hotel recognized that these are the guys who talk to tourists about where to eat, where to gamble, and where to shop. Before the hotel officially opened, it gave this high-powered group of talkers free rooms and the run of the place. Which hotel do you think the cabbies are talking about now?

Talkers Are People Like Us

There's a myth that word of mouth is only spread by über-hip talkers and the cool trendsetters described in Malcolm Gladwell's book *The Tipping Point*. Consultants who sell trend-spotting services have perpetuated this impression. Reporters love to write about the super-cool, celebrities, and opinion leaders. But that's not what most word of mouth is about.

Remember what you've learned—consumers turn to people like us. They don't need a paid celebrity endorser (or a celebrity who has been paid off with free merchandise) to tell them what to buy. They want to hear from someone with the same needs and lifestyle that they have. I never could quite figure out why anyone would be influenced by Michael Jordan's endorsement of Rayovac batteries. Does he use a lot of AAs?

Of course, there are the professionals—the doctors, lawyers, accountants, and electricians—whose advice and recommendations carry the weight of their formal credentials. But most talkers are ordinary, everyday people of all ages, interests, incomes, and status levels.

One active PTA mom recommends more products in a week than any club hopper.

Your talkers are the people who are sending you new customers. Here are some examples:

- Current customers
- The worker who gets a flyer in the mail and hands it to a colleague
- People who post reviews online
- People in the neighborhood
- A shopper who helps another shopper in the aisle

Discovering the talkers for your stuff is sometimes easy—but sometimes, it takes a little ingenuity.

One of the best examples of an organization finding its talkers is The Prostate Net, a nonprofit committed to educating minority men about the risks of prostate cancer and the importance of getting exams. (An awkward conversation, to say the least.)

They created a word of mouth program called the "Barbershop Network." Barbers are the opinion leaders in many communities, and they have the time to talk to their clients—they're perfect talkers. The group reached out to 50,000 barbers, taught them how to talk to their clients about the issue, and provided educational resources to pass along.

They put the Five Ts of word of mouth marketing into practice. They identified the talkers (barbers); the topic (the importance of prostate exams); the tool (informational brochures and other educational resources); took part (establishing a dialog with the barbers); and tracked the results (frequency of prostate exams).

This solid talker program is so much better than what a traditional ad agency would have come up with—probably some cheesy public service announcement.

Talkers Aren't Always Big Spenders

Lots of businesses think that their talkers are the customers who shop most often or spend the most money. That's often not the case. Just because someone is buying doesn't mean that she's also talking.

Your best talker might be your newest customer.

Think about when you talk about restaurants. You probably never tell anyone about the place you go every week or the place you stop at for coffee on the way to work. Your favorite joint is so much a part of your everyday life that, like most people, you probably rarely think to mention it to anyone.

But what do you do when you go to a new restaurant for the first time? You tell everyone you see the next day. Your friends, family, and coworkers. And a week later, you've probably forgotten all about it.

Your most active, powerful advocates may be the ones who have done business with you only once. They are excited about the experience. They like the product. And they're in a honeymoon period where everything is still great.

You need to think fast—you've got to turn these brand-new customers into talkers on their very first visit. What remarkable experience can you give them to pump up their word of mouth activities?

The lesson: Don't just dig into your customer database and assume that the active customers or big spenders are your talkers. Make sure that you've found the real talkers.

FIND YOUR TALKERS

Everything starts with the right talkers.

Each group of talkers will have a different set of interests. Figure out who they are and what pumps them up. Once you know your target talkers, you'll know which topics they like, which tools to use, and how to join in the conversation.

Here are the most common types of talkers.

Talkers #1: Happy Customers

The most familiar talkers are the happy customers you already have.

You know them: those customers who are just so pleased with what you do that they want everyone to do business with you. These are the people who love to tell their friends about you, who mention you first when someone asks about a business like yours. The trick is to learn to separate the customers who are just satisfied from those who are eager to talk.

To Find Them: Learn to look for signs of extreme enthusiasm. Look for customers who come back frequently, who learn the names of the employees, and who are bubbling with enthusiasm.

Be sure your sales team learns to look for these signs. It's easy to get annoyed with overeager customers; instead, appreciate that their enthusiasm is a major word of mouth asset.

Pay attention to people who fill out comment cards, sign up for newsletters, submit suggestions online, comment on your message boards, or email you. All of these are signs that the person feels a greater connection than a regular shopper. Pay attention to customer surveys and referral programs. A lot of businesses ask, "How did you hear about us?" but rarely do anything with the information. The answer to that question may be the name of your new talker.

Talkers #2: Online Talkers

Look for people who have posted a comment about you on a website somewhere. Look for reviews, raves, and responses.

The fact that someone wrote about you at all is a major step. Most people are too busy to do something like this. It shows a special interest in your stuff if someone has the time and personality to post a review. Look for these people because they have the extra motivation that takes them from being a consumer to being a talker.

To Find Them: Use the search engines, both a regular one and a specialized one that searches the blogs. When you find these talkers, go ahead and make a list. Feel free to email them and introduce yourself, but do *not* spam them.

Talkers #3: Logo Lovers

This one is so easy that it hurts.

Anyone who wears your logo is a talker. Hat, shirt, bag, whatever. These are the people who like you so much that they will advertise your brand for free. Do whatever you can to identify and encourage them.

There is a very simple reason why people wear logos: They want to show that they are part of your group of fans. The need to belong is powerful.

To Find Them: Make it easy for people to ask for logo items and track who's asking. These are very active talkers.

Logo lovers can't show their support if you don't give them a chance. Give out goodies with your logo. Create an online store with a full line of logo gear (try CafePress.com to get a custom clothing store up in less than an hour).

Talkers #4: Eager Employees

Even your employees can be effective talkers.

Assuming you're a good company, many will have a pride in what they do that is easily transmitted to potential new customers. Not every employee wants to be a talker. But you can identify those with that special team spirit that makes them ideal word of mouth spreaders.

Cold Stone Creamery found that some of its most eager talkers are the high school kids who work behind the counter mixing its fantastic ice cream. They have eagerness and enthusiasm for the store, plus the status and inside knowledge that make them great talkers. It translates into word of mouth energy broadcast to all their friends—legions of hungry teenagers—keeping the chain buzzworthy among a key customer group.

To Find Them: First, look around. The right employee talkers will be fairly self-evident. They will be the ones with bumper stickers on their cars and briefcases with your logo. We had a new employee who was so excited about joining the company that he sent our electronic brochure to everyone in his online network on his first day of work.

Talkers #5: Listeners

People who listen are often the people who talk the most.

Look for the people who are eager to get information about your company. Someone who cares enough to subscribe to your newsletter is hungry to know the latest news. A lot of them will be talkers who want great info nuggets that they can pass along.

To Find Them: Pay attention to your subscriber lists. Use an email-delivery company that lets you track who forwards your newsletters—those are active talkers.

Talkers #6: Fans and Hobbyists

The most hyperactive talkers are often die-hard fans and hobbyists.

Chanel and Gucci didn't build their brands on just the ultrarich who wear their products. They did it with word of mouth from millions of fans who dream about being able to afford them some day. These eager enthusiasts can become active talkers. Many products—cars, computers, music, movies, and anything fashion based—have a similar fan base.

Even the most humdrum products have crazy fans. A guy named Matt Galloway started an intense, detailed blog about the obscure details of word of mouth marketing research methodology. Not exciting, unless you're really into it. He doesn't work in the business, and he's not even a researcher. He just likes to talk about the topic. (It just goes to prove that there's a fan for everything.)

Word of mouth also can be a hobby for certain people. A woman named Harriet Klausner likes to write book reviews. She has a background in library science and has worked at several bookstores. She's posted more than 11,000 reviews on Amazon. Just for fun. Harriet is a talker.

To Find Them: Fans are easy to find—they almost always have websites these days.

Talkers #7: Professionals

There is a special class of talkers who do it for a living: reporters, columnists, critics, full-time bloggers, business networkers, and a whole variety of authors and experts.

Dealing with professional talkers is where we cross into what most people consider the job of the public relations department. Amateur talkers (real consumers) are the focus of this book, but many of the techniques that apply to them also impact what the professionals say.

Special rules apply to these talkers. For most of them, objectivity and evenhandedness are paramount. They're expected to know what they're talking about and will take a credibility hit if they pass along bunk. They have a right to be suspicious and skeptical of your claims, and they won't tend to get overly excited about new products.

But their caution also makes their recommendation more desirable. The professionals we trust earn that trust by being honest and smart. And, because of their reach, they can be catalysts for word of mouth. Particularly for brands that are not well known, being talked about in an influential newsletter, mentioned in a well-linked blog, or featured in a magazine review can be the nudge that gets the positive word of mouth rolling.

Oprah Winfrey is probably the most powerful professional talker in the world right now. Whether it's a casual mention or one of her formal endorsements (like her book club or annual "Favorite Things" episodes), her word of mouth usually equals instant stardom.

HOW TO RECOGNIZE GOOD TALKERS

Talkers aren't all the same. Some people talk to a few friends; some talk to everyone on the planet. Some are convincing; some are full of hot air.

Once you've found a group of talkers, you can look further for the signs that some of them will be extra helpful. Great talkers share these traits.

Passion. They are excited about your stuff, and they are generally excited about life. True talkers are optimistic and enthusiastic and just love to share their energy. We all know this sort of person—the one who just can't help talking about the new, cool thing that she just discovered.

This doesn't mean that you're looking only for chatty teenagers. You're looking for people who care about the topic, invest their time in it, and have strong opinions. Think "dedicated hobbyist." A true foodie isn't making unsolicited calls to tell his friends about restaurants, but he cares deeply about where to eat. Ask him a question, and you'll get recommendations, reviews, and strong opinions about where to get a meal.

Credibility. It doesn't much matter if the cashier at a drugstore recommends a painkiller. You'd rather listen to the pharmacist. Each of them probably talks to the same number of people in a day, but the pharmacist has the reputation to back up the recommendation.

This doesn't mean that talkers must have professional credentials; they just need to have some expertise in what they are talking about. You wouldn't ask your friend the pizza fiend about fine dining, but you would trust his advice about where to go for great deep-dish (and a good beer). When you're looking for good talkers, look for those who are devoted enough to the topic to impress others. Often, just being a consumer is enough: If I wear fashionable clothes, people will ask me about fashion.

Connection. Talkers have much more impact when they have a wide network of people they talk to. You want to look for talkers who are members of clubs or associations, who volunteer, who are on a team, or who have public jobs. Quantity often counts when it comes to word of mouth.

Look for certain behaviors that indicate that someone has a sharing personality. Look for indications of how involved and communicative they are: Do they post photos online, have an Amazon wish list, volunteer, or write a blog? Look for members of groups that are actually created for the purpose of spreading word of mouth. For example, Business Network International has more than 84,000 members who meet to share sales leads and word of mouth.

Travelers are one highly connected bunch of talkers, especially business travelers. They obviously are going to see someone (to whom they will talk) and are possibly going to a large meeting or major convention (where they will talk to a lot of people). Cosmetics companies pay to get their soaps and lotions stocked in the rooms of the best hotels. Food companies want airlines to give out their new snacks. They want to get their products into the hands of talkers who are on their way to a talking experience.

YOUR TALKER PROFILE

Now that you've got a sense of who is talking about you, narrow it down.

Your next steps are to:

1. Pick a single group of talkers you want to work with

2. Create a plan to reach them

You can't deliver a good word of mouth marketing program that tries to be all things to all people. What motivates one group of talkers will be very different from what motivates another.

If you have found multiple sets of good talkers, that's great. Just go through the Five Ts and create a unique program for each group.

Build a Talker Profile

Write a one-page memo that describes your talkers and why they want to talk. This is your Talker Profile. Don't get fancy. You'll use this to keep you focused while you're planning your word of mouth campaign.

Here's what you should ask in the Talker Profile:

• Who are the talkers?

• What are their basic characteristics?

• What are they already talking about?

• Whom are they talking to?

• How do you contact them?

Here's an example for a day care center.

Talker Profile for
ABC Day Care Center

Who They Are: Working parents

Characteristics: These moms and dads are busy professionals who drop off their kids at our day care center. They are dual-career couples with active work and social lives. They like day care because they can continue their active lives while knowing that their kids are being cared for and educated.

They Talk About: Child care issues, specifically work/life balance issues. They always want to know how to do more with their kids and still get some time for activities without their kids. They like day care because of the freedom it gives them, so they are talking it up.

They Talk To: Other parents, usually in their neighborhood or in the workplace, or to family members. They are also the first to give advice to expecting parents. Some of them have blogs or family websites.

How to Contact Them: We see them every day when they drop off their kids, and we can email them directly.

You can see how this simple exercise starts you thinking about how to work with these particular talkers.

Let's continue with this example. Our day care center wants to enroll more children. We know that our talkers are talking to their neighbors and coworkers, many of whom have kids and child care issues. We could create a word of mouth campaign around a simple idea designed to appeal specifically to these talkers—an after-work babysitting program. If parents could leave their kids at day care for an extra few hours and go to dinner, they would be telling everyone at work about it. In contrast, had our talkers been grandparents, we might have chosen an entirely different topic.

On the opposite page is a blank form for you to complete the exercise for yourself.

Build a Contact Plan

Now that you know who your talkers are, you need a way to talk to them.

Don't let them get away without opening up some channel of communication. If you can't reach them regularly, then you have no way to influence the word of mouth conversation. The ability to talk to the talkers is one of the key concepts that separates word of mouth *marketing* from conversations that happen without your involvement.

Here are the basic steps to take when you find a talker.

Step #1: Get Permission and Contact Information.
When someone in a store shows enthusiasm, ask if you can put her on a VIP list. Offer a coupon or some other special if you need to. When someone writes about you online, ask him if he'd like to get insider news in the future.

Don't forget to get contact information. It's hard to talk to them if you don't know how to reach them.

Be careful and polite. Remember that everyone is nervous about getting spammed, and most people are suspicious about any business that wants to contact them.

But don't be shy. If you've done a good job of identifying your talkers, then they should be enthusiastic to hear from you. The right people will be eager to get the latest scoop.

Talker Profile For: _____

Who They Are: _____
_____
_____
_____
_____
_____

Characteristics: _____
_____
_____
_____
_____
_____

They Talk About: _____
_____
_____
_____
_____
_____

They Talk To: _____
_____
_____
_____
_____
_____

How to Contact Them: _____
_____
_____
_____
_____
_____

Step #2: Create a Contact Vehicle. Design an email newsletter, chat room, blog, or paper newsletter just for your talkers. You can't call them up every time you have a new topic to talk about. You need a simple, ongoing message-delivery system that they can tune into.

Blogs can come in very handy. Many talkers won't want to be on a subscription list, but they will check in with your blog on a regular basis.

It doesn't really matter how you plan to connect with your talkers—just make sure you can.

FEED YOUR TALKERS

Talkers live on a diet of information. Keep them fed to keep them talking. The word of mouth stops when there is nothing to talk about.

Talkers want to know what's going on. They want the latest gossip. They want to know what's happening before anyone else does. Talkers maintain their expertise and status by being well informed and educated about your products.

Create a steady stream of exclusive information for your talkers. It doesn't matter how you deliver this information. Blogs and email newsletters are nice, but get the information out there any way you can. Just be sure that your talkers are the first to see it.

The off-Broadway hit musical *Altar Boyz* emails a thank-you note to its audience members after each show. The message also has a special coupon for the talkers to share, giving them the chance to look good to their friends. The email links them to a website full of goodies to talk about. Photos, downloads, fun postings from the audience, newsletters, and all the usual stuff. The more information you give the talkers, the more they will talk.

Here is what talkers want to see.

- *Detailed data.* You'll be surprised at how much of what you think of as mundane is of great interest to your fans. Talkers are hungry for detail. Share technical data and product manuals. Get geeky.

- *Progress reports.* Talk about new products in development, future menu items, or next season's plans. Let them know what you're working on.

- *Company news.* Remember, talkers want to be family members. Fill them in on the personalities and happenings in your office, the new hires, promotions, and anniversaries. Put a human face on your operation.

A Lesson from Charities—Motivating Talkers

Businesses can take a lesson from grassroots organizations. Charities, politicians, and volunteer organizations are great at keeping talkers happy. It's what they do best.

Volunteer motivation and management are what makes these groups tick, and they have developed a whole science around it. Every good volunteer manager knows the rules for keeping volunteers happy.

- *Always say yes to a volunteer.* You can walk into any political campaign without an appointment and offer to volunteer, and there will always be a project waiting for you. The secret? Campaigns always save some work for volunteers. For example, when they send out a big direct mail campaign, they always leave a stack of envelopes to be stamped and sealed by hand. *Have something ready when your talkers are ready.*

- *Make them feel important.* Find a way to make them feel like an insider (and look like one to their friends). A political candidate shakes as many hands in the office as on the campaign trail. I still get a holiday card every year from the senator for whom I volunteered in 1988. *Show that you appreciate the talkers.*

- *Make it fun.* Why in the world do we have those walkathons with the rigmarole of getting per-mile pledges? Isn't there an easier way to raise money than selling cookies? It's because these gimmicks are a lot more fun than going door to door with a tin cup. *Make talking entertaining and challenging.*

- *Throw good parties.*

Family Guy: A Little Attention Goes a Long Way

There's no better example of the power of taking care of your talkers than the revival of the television show *Family Guy*. The hysterically funny cartoon was pulled by FOX after just two seasons. The following year, FOX launched a word of mouth campaign to promote the show's DVD.

It didn't take long to find the talkers. Hundreds of fan sites were devoted to the show—a real labor of love in the days before blogs, when building a website required buying a domain, hosting, and all the other hassles. These webmasters were special, willing to devote real effort to talking up a show they loved.

These talkers were given *status* and *recognition* with a club created for them called the Online Team. Team members were given exclusive access to a private website with show clips, audio files, downloadable icons, private emails, and merchandise. They were given a mission—to recruit more team members. They felt very, very special.

These efforts made them into even more powerful talkers. The exclusive content gave them lots to talk about. All that content also made their websites richer and more interesting. Those little fan sites grew into hubs for thousands of new visitors.

The result? What started as a DVD sales effort turned into a word of mouth movement that did something that has rarely happened in the history of television—the cancelled show went back into production and new episodes were put on the air.

The campaign website still remains the link between the show and its fans, who continue to receive all sorts of benefits from continually spreading word of mouth.

SAY THANK YOU

One tool is more powerful than all the others (your folks taught you this one): Say thank you.

Get good at making your talkers feel appreciated and recognized. They will talk 10 times as often. You can never say thank you enough, and every thanks is a reason for them to talk even more.

All these talkers are advertising for you, for free. They are supporting your business, bringing in customers, and increasing your profits. These people are out there singing your praises and putting their names on the line for you.

They deserve a little thanks—and, conveniently, thanks is all they want in return for their hard work.

They feel like part of the family. A pat on the back from the company (or even a simple acknowledgment that you know that they exist) is like receiving praise from a parent. So don't be stingy.

I'm not talking about gifts, compensation, or cash rewards. I'm talking about *recognition* and *gratitude*. The core motivations that get people to spread the word about you are driven by deep-seated emotional desires to connect with you. A little acknowledgment and a thank you are what they need to cement that emotional connection.

Thank Them Personally

Get in the habit of saying thank you. Say it face to face when you see your talkers. Send thank-you notes. I send more than 100 thank-you notes each month, and they work. Snapshots of my notes are actually posted to a few blogs, and I get a surprising number of thanks in return. It says something about society that so few people get a thank you that it's worth writing about on a website.

The salespeople at Allen-Edmonds shoes send a handwritten thank-you note every time I call and order shoes by phone. I even get a note when I buy from the discount outlet store.

It is important to say a special thanks if you can connect a talker to a specific piece of new business. Take the time to do something to acknowledge that you appreciate what that talker did for you. Web hosting company MediaTemple sent me a credit for a month's free service in exchange for referring a customer. I didn't even know that it was coming, and I never signed up for any sort of rewards program. The gift was that much more appreciated.

A great way to thank a bunch of people at once is through special, exclusive benefits. Give them a permanent discount. Send them samples of new products or give them dibs on closeouts. Let them tour the factory. Find creative ways to make your talkers feel appreciated. Talkers who get a cool experience tell everyone about it.

Thank Them Publicly

Recognition is more powerful when it's public.

Think about the awesome power of the high scores list on a video game. A lot of quarters went into Pac-Man machines to get on that list.

Mention your top talkers on your website. Put up a public thank-you page to acknowledge people who have done you a favor. Put your favorite talkers' photos on the wall and their names on a plaque. Frame all the thank-you letters that you get. Give thanks in your newsletters.

On your blog, give prominent links to people who post comments or link back to you. The blog culture is all about mutual recognition, so your thanks will be paid back. On your message board, give the talkers a flashy icon. Find those super-energetic writers and give them special status. Make them look and feel important.

There's a reason why many companies give the best parking space to the salesperson of the month—everyone can see it.

Make Recognition Part of the Program

eBay does a better job than anyone of making recognition part of the fundamental structure of its service. Everyone who has any interaction with the company gets status. Logos, icons, and enhancements show everyone that the active contributors are special.

With a little creativity, you can build similar automatic recognition into your word of mouth program. Create a way to acknowledge talkers wherever they interact with other people. Give them a logo to put on their website.

Membership organizations love to give out membership plaques and lapel pins so their members stand out from the crowd. At conferences, they give out tons of special buttons, ribbons, and rewards to recognize the most important talkers.

Lifeway Christian Resources was selling a new Bible-study course online. It wanted to motivate and recognize its talkers. It created a fantastic tell-a-friend page that let you send an ecard to friends. Senders also entered the country where their friends lived. Each sender was given a web page with a map of the world—with a pin in the map for each country where they sent an ecard. Here's where it gets cool: When recipients sent ecards to *their* friends, the original senders got more pins on *their* maps. Senders could literally see how they were spreading the word around the world. This clever tool gave great recognition to the original senders, gave them a clear sense of the impact of their word of mouth, and was good fun. As you can imagine, many talkers became extremely active, trying to find new ways to get more pins in their maps.

CREATE A TALKER PROGRAM

One of the established techniques for connecting with your talkers is to create a formal talker program. This is some sort of official membership group that your company creates to bring talkers together and to give them recognition and status.

A good talker program can be simple. All you need is:

- A web page
- A way to sign up
- Benefits for participation
- A newsletter

If you put these pieces together, you get a home base for your most active talkers that provides both a means of recognition and a communications hub to feed them information.

These programs are often called "evangelism" or "ambassador" programs—but you probably know them by their original name: the fan club.

Fan Clubs

Fan clubs may be the first formal word of mouth marketing programs. Think of 1950s teenyboppers, screaming at the top of their lungs and sending in 50 cents to join the Buddy Holly Fan Club. These days, you see the exact same thing at hyperspeed, powered by instant online communications.

You can have a fan club for anything. Even WD-40.

The official WD-40 Fan Club is amazing. Members get exclusive content, tips and tricks, and lots of fun. They get a weekly newsletter, a membership card, screen savers, and video games they can download. The members even elected an honorary board of directors.

Every bit of it is completely fun—and it's a perfect way to involve, energize, and reward talkers.

Another favorite is the Fisk-a-Teers, a fan club sponsored by Fiskars, the scissors manufacturer. You wouldn't think that scissors are that exciting, but when you combine it with the massive craze for scrapbooking, you've got people who care about what they use to cut paper. It's a full-fledged fan club with blogs, message boards, and more.

One website, lots of happy talkers.

Ambassador Programs

Maker's Mark bourbon whiskey has a very sophisticated ambassador program that takes its relationship with talkers to the next level. In addition to giving its talkers a way of identifying themselves to the company, it encourages its ambassadors to talk about the product and rewards them for being an active part of the community.

When you sign up to be a Maker's Mark Ambassador, you get tons of care and attention. You get your name on an aging barrel of bourbon. You get personal emails from the CEO, invitations to private parties around the country, bar glasses, holiday cards to send to your friends, and (of course) the status that comes from being a member of the family.

Maker's Mark whiskey realized that its customers have a greater appreciation for handcrafted bourbon than the typical whiskey consumer and that their connoisseurship is something they want to share with others. They have crafted a fun pledge that simultaneously flatters their talkers and asks them to get out and start talking:

I, as a Maker's Mark Ambassador, do pledge to introduce those who have not yet had the pleasure (poor souls) to the smooth taste of Maker's Mark bourbon. To help friends understand, appreciate, and savor what handmade bourbon is all about. To encourage establishments I encounter within my travels to stock Maker's Mark for their thirsty patrons. And to lead by my own example, that every occasion for enjoying bourbon is the perfect occasion for enjoying Maker's Mark.

That pledge pretty much sums up what talkers are all about.

Customer Advisory Boards

For more conservative companies, you can create a "customer advisory board." This is a formal program in which customers are invited to give feedback to the company. Sometimes these are small programs with 15 to 20 participants, but you can use the web to open the program up to all of your talkers. Customer advisory boards give you a way to talk to your talkers without explicitly asking them to talk for you.

A program like this has two simple benefits. First, it gets you lots of great customer feedback. Second, it opens up the door for lots of talkers to feel a connection to the company. It gives them a way to participate. And, of course, people who feel appreciated are likely to tell their friends about you.

RALLY THE FAITHFUL

Customers who are devoted to your stuff love getting together with other people who are just as devoted. People who share the love of a brand are part of an extended family.

So have a family reunion.

It turns isolated talkers into a word of mouth army.

Harley-Davidson asks on its website: "Who says you can't choose your family?" And they deliver, by creating the Harley Owners Group, the gold standard for connecting talkers in the real world. The club has more than one million members in more than 1,000 chapters. Its mission is a simple one: to ride and have fun.

Harley owners take pride in their bikes and look for any excuse to talk about them. Harley gives them that excuse in the form of dozens of statewide and national rallies every year. More than 500,000 people attend the big annual rally in Sturgis, South Dakota. Every gathering supercharges their enthusiasm and gives them something new to talk about.

But you don't need to have the fanatical devotion that Harley-Davidson enjoys to create a space in which your talkers can connect. Software companies hold developer conferences where programmers and others get together to talk about technical advances in the software, learn, network, and self-reinforce their loyalty to the product.

Microsoft hosts more than 150 live events in a typical month. If these meetings were just about training, the courses could be taught online. But an important purpose is to get talkers together, get them pumped up, and give them a reason to talk about their favorite products.

Getting these people together creates enthusiasm in the community. Let's face it, a lot of programmers lead a solitary existence at work, so getting 30 firewall administrators together makes them feel like part of a greater whole. If they make a connection to the others in the group (and have some fun), they will want to attend the next meeting, which means that they will stick with the software. And it guarantees that they'll be spreading great word of mouth about the product.

The life of an eBay seller working from home can be lonely, too. So the company brings them all together once a year in an amazing 10,000-person convention/party/reunion/festival called eBay Live! It is an amazing gathering of ultra-energized people who are thrilled to meet their fellow sellers for the first time. It's a bonding experience.

While the official purpose of the event is to learn skills to be a more effective seller, the real purpose is to generate enthusiasm. Between sessions, attendees wear silly hats, swap collectible pins, and attend the official eBay dance. There was even an eBay community cookbook this year. Those attendees come home giddy with enthusiasm for the brand and become stellar talkers.

Simple Events to Keep People Talking

You don't need a convention to make this work for you. Just think about the easiest way to get your talkers together.

If you have a store, host a cocktail party, live music, or a book reading. It doesn't matter what the reason is; just create an excuse to invite everyone over. For years, I've traveled around the country hosting a series of networking dinners called the "Feast for Smart Marketers." There's not much to it—I book a Chinese banquet hall and invite everyone I know in town. No speaker, no panel discussion. Just 200 people and lots of great food. Pretty much all of my customers and lots of great word of mouth come from these simple dinners.

CHAPTER FIVE

Topics: What Will They Talk About?

YOUR JOB: GIVE PEOPLE SOMETHING TO TALK ABOUT

All word of mouth starts with a topic of conversation. People won't talk about you if you don't give them something to say.

Anything that catches attention is a topic. Anything that catches attention and then gets talked about is a fantastic topic.

All sorts of things can be good topics: The cow-decorated boxes that hold Gateway computers, a fabulous freebie, a moment of great customer service, a special dessert, or an unusual advertisement.

Zappos, an online shoe store, provides a no-questions-asked, 365-day return policy. Yep, you can keep the shoes for a year before returning them. I doubt anyone returns their shoes that late, but it is a fantastic reason to talk.

It's Not Your Mission Statement

A word of mouth topic is not your official marketing message or your formal brand statement. It's a simple message that sparks interest and conversation.

Great word of mouth topics are often hard for traditional marketers to see. They violate the rules of marketing. They aren't planned, they aren't corporate, and they are rarely official. It's an exception when real people want to repeat your official company motto or carefully crafted theme. Instead, people latch onto the *unexpected*.

RedEnvelope is an online gift catalog. They have nice stuff but not necessarily nicer than any other good catalog. Their motto: "RedEnvelope's mission is to make gift giving, no matter what the occasion or circumstance, simple and fun." That's fine, but nobody is going to repeat it.

But they have a killer topic: Every item comes gift wrapped in the most gorgeous, elegant, impressive red box with a giant bow. People who receive gifts from them can't help but talk about the wrapping. (They talk about the wrapping more than the gifts.)

The wrapping is a perfect word of mouth topic. It makes people want to talk, and it's easy to talk about. When most people get a gift from a catalog, they rarely remember the catalog, just the item and who sent it. RedEnvelope's box creates instant word of mouth. When one of those boxes is opened at a party or a baby shower, a whole roomful of people are talking about it.

Every company, every product has at least one great topic. Your job is to find it and give people something to talk about.

Now, to be totally honest, sometimes finding a topic is pure luck. You'll try a lot of things; you'll put out some interesting ideas. No one will talk about what you ask them to, and everyone will start talking about something completely different.

FINDING A GREAT TOPIC

Don't overthink this. The topic that works best for you will be something so simple, and possibly silly, that you may miss it. Good word of mouth topics are the kind of great, easy ideas that get buried by bureaucracy in a corporate planning session.

Lower the bar, keep your mind open, and expect that it may be your intern who comes up with the most amazing word of mouth topic.

There are three rules to developing a great topic: keep it simple, organic, and portable.

Good Topics Are Simple

Keep your topic short and sweet. It should be developed around a single idea that's easy to repeat.

A few hotels have begun to figure this out. The Hotel Monaco chain wants to be thought of as cool and fun. So they offer each guest an in-room goldfish. That's something you tell a friend. Westin did years of research to create the Heavenly Bed, a bed so nice that you'll talk about it the next day. (Every other chain has copied them, so they need a new topic.) Quiznos is giving Subway a run for its money with the idea of hot, toasty subs. Even though Subway always had them, Quiznos pulled it to the front as a topic of conversation.

If you're a cheesehead like me (a Wisconsinite), then you love cheese curds, little lumps of cheddar that are squeaky when they are fresh. During a car trip though central Wisconsin, my wife and I drove past a giant billboard with the words "Squeaky Curds" and an exit number. Must . . . get . . . curds.

Twenty miles later, we ended up at the Carr Valley Cheese factory in tiny La Valle, Wisconsin. We had some curds. They were amazing, fresh, and oh-so-squeaky.

They also had unbelievable, rare, and ultra-gourmet prize-winning cheeses. The kind that you only find at exclusive cheese shops. We bought a ton. We sent some to a friend who is a New York City chef. We've turned into true talkers.

But when we talk, we talk about their squeaky curds. We've brought a lot of people to the store, and we've sent a lot of mail-order gifts. You can't explain a great half-sheep, half-goat smoked feta as easily as you can say, "You gotta try these curds."

Carr Valley Cheese picked its topic correctly.

A great topic is more basic than you think. Resist the urge to make it complicated.

Good Topics Are Organic

Good *organic* topics are based on the exceptional qualities that make your stuff stand out. It's about being buzzworthy. These are usually the most sustainable topics around.

> **Big Idea: Word of mouth is as much about product features as it is about marketing.**

Design and features are worth talking about. They provide topics that flow naturally from the products' attributes, without much need to be pushed by marketing.

If you want long-term, deep-seated word of mouth that creates a fantastic brand, then you need more than a one-off promotion. You need to work to create products that people fall in love with and are compelled to share with their friends.

What are you doing that's worth talking about?

Good Topics Are Portable

You need a topic that's easy to move along.

Entrepreneurs are always looking for an elevator pitch, which is a story you can tell an investor while in the elevator of a 20-story building. That's way too long for word of mouth.

You need the pass-in-the-hall test. Try to fill in the blanks with your stuff:

"You should try _____, it's _____."

"Can you believe _____ did _____?"

"There's nothing better than _____ for _____."

There should never be an *and* anywhere near your topic. Topics don't work as well when they become lists. ("Try us because we're friendly, affordable, experienced, have great customer service, and give you free ice cream while you wait.") Your topic should be repeatable within a second or so. ("We give you free ice cream while you wait.") Otherwise, no one will remember it.

Amazing Topics Are Unexpected

Listen very carefully to your customers. They are probably already talking about something—and it may not be what you were expecting.

That's okay. Go with it.

Whatever gets your customers excited is a great topic. Don't worry if your marketing plan says to promote speed, and people are talking about price instead. Don't panic if your exciting stain remover turns out to be a great weed killer.

Hidden features and unexpected uses are one of the best word of mouth topics you'll ever get. (Your advertising people will get grouchy and try to squash this organic message for a canned one that they created. Ignore them.) If people are talking about something unexpected, it's not wrong—it's an opportunity.

Did you know that kids are making prom dresses and tuxedos out of duct tape? This is a great word of mouth topic that was totally unexpected.

Duck Tape brand duct tape spotted the fad and encouraged it. They now have an annual "Stuck at Prom" contest to award college scholarships to the most creative couples. More than 250 couples entered the contest in 2005, representing thousands of hours of work and an immense amount of word of mouth. Check out the winners at *www.stuckatprom.com*—and see how many people you tell.

TAKING CARE OF YOUR TOPICS

It's not over after you've found a topic. You need to keep improving it and massaging it to make sure it stays relevant and effective.

Test Your Topic

The only way to know if you've found a good topic is by trying it out in the real world. No amount of planning will help you know in advance. Test it. It's a good topic if it works.

Here are some tests to see if your topic is ready to fly:

- *The telephone game.* Can your topic get passed along from person to person at least three times and come back to you recognizable?

- *The high-school test.* Ask a teenager if you're buzzworthy. A glimmer of interest means that you're on to something good.

- *The customer test.* Leak your topic to a customer or two and watch what happens. Do they respond to it? Do they repeat it? Does anyone new come into the store and ask you about the topic?

Keep It Fresh

Topics do go stale after a while.

Unfortunately, the more people talk about something, the less interesting it is. Success can eat away at a topic's effectiveness, because the motivation for word of mouth is often to share inside information. When was the last time someone told you about the exciting new iPod?

I helped promote a new marketing conference primarily using word of mouth. We had great success with a companion blog and podcast that featured interviews with all the speakers before the event. It was original and widely talked about.

So we did it again—and results were disappointing. Everyone already knew about the blog and podcast, so there was no reason to talk about them. We're looking for a new topic.

Don't Drop Your Topic

Here's something to watch out for. Once you have a successful topic that is creating good word of mouth, you have to keep it up. Your commitment to the topic will set you apart just as much as the topic itself. And, should you ever stop doing whatever you were doing to get attention, people will notice.

How much do you like the Milwaukee airport? Would you stop there even if you didn't have to?

Midwest Airlines had a good thing going with two strong topics and a devoted following because of them. The airline provided first-class-style seating at coach fares. Every person on board was treated like a high-status passenger, from the amazing meals served on china to the cushy, two-across, big leather seats throughout the cabin. Topic number two was pretty cool, too. They baked chocolate chip cookies on board every flight.

And really, who doesn't like being treated like a first-class flyer? Who doesn't like fresh-baked cookies? People loved it, talked about it, and started to opt for an extra stop in Milwaukee (Midwest's hub) just to get on board.

Then Midwest launched its Saver Service, offering clients coach seating and lower fares. No leather, no china, only occasional cookies. Customers who wanted to pay more for all the previously standard bells and whistles could still do so. But, of course, people wanting to pay more for first-class treatment can do that with any airline.

Midwest found a way to cut costs, and they cut out the topic that was the basis for their stellar word of mouth. No one is talking about them anymore.

STEP 1: FIND A TOPIC YOU CAN USE TODAY

I promised from the beginning that you'd get word of mouth strategies that would get people talking right away. Here they are.

These are simple things you can do to get people talking immediately, without spending a lot of money and without fundamentally changing your business. (Keep reading for some more sophisticated topics that require a bit more effort.)

Special Sales

The easiest topic you could possibly create is a good sale or special offer. You could put down this book, discount a favorite product, throw a sign up in the window, and someone will tell their friends. It doesn't take a lot of finesse to bring people in and get them talking about a sale. Sales are a long-proven word of mouth topic.

Although sales won't keep people talking forever, they create bursts of conversation.

Give it a little extra oomph by coming up with an unusual offer. A buy-one, get-something-not-normally-for-sale offer, something crazy, or a catchy theme. You can get a lot of conversations going with a creative message.

Keep the word of mouth moving with the sure-thing tool of exclusivity, or even just the appearance of exclusivity. These days, it's common to get an email with a "secret" discount coupon supposedly just for friends and family of employees. Of course, these are designed to leak out and spread across the web. So create a special offer, put it in an email, and ask your employees to share it with their friends. Employees will be happy to be talkers, and they get the status of being able to hook up their friends with a deal. Word of mouth will take care of the rest.

Extraordinary Customer Service

"They treat me well" is an awfully powerful word of mouth topic. Nice guys, in this case, finish first.

It's not hard to get noticed when you do something special for your customers, because very few companies bother. With so little remarkable customer service these days, anything generous, respectful, or creative will get talked about.

The great thing about terrific customer service is that it works for every type of business.

The handyman who takes his shoes off every time he enters your house or the delivery people who willingly dispose of your old stuff get extra credit for themselves and generate solid word of mouth for their companies. You're more likely to refer your friends to movers who deliver extra boxes to you, to self-storage places that offer a free loaner truck, or to the Realtor who sat at your new house and waited for furniture to be delivered.

LensCrafters fixes glasses for free, even if they were bought somewhere else. Headsets.com, a $30 million online store, sends a thank-you email after each order—with the direct phone number and email for the CEO. Sears lets you return or exchange major appliances, no questions asked, within 90 days. That's a big deal if the refrigerator that looked great in the store looks terrible in your kitchen. These little extras earn extra word of mouth.

PrintingforLess.com has become one of the most popular printing companies in America through extraordinary customer service. I recently ordered a small batch of brochures. They actually went to my website and noticed that the logo on the brochure was a slightly different color than the one on my website. They called to make sure it was okay. Then they fixed it for free. All that service for an order worth less than $500. As you can imagine, they get a ton of word of mouth from my team.

Look at your customer service from a word of mouth perspective. Are you set up to give people a reason to talk? Or a reason to talk negatively? When someone gets off the phone with your company, what will they tell their friends?

Think about those little extra things you can do to make people talk about you.

Do Something Silly

Businesses are way too serious these days.

Make people smile and they will talk about you. Humor may be the best medicine—it's also a super word of mouth topic.

Do you feel an emotional attachment to your backpack? Jan-Sport knows that a lot of people do and offers them a very special lifetime warranty. You don't send your bags in for repairs. You send them to "Backpack Camp" for a little vacation. You even get a cute postcard from your bag, telling you all about the fun it is having at camp and letting you know when it's coming home.

Sometimes the silliest topics arise from product names themselves. Is there anything amusing or memorable about foundation repair? Not unless you're dealing with The Crack Team, a St. Louis-based company that is widely known because of a beloved mascot, Mr. Happy Crack, and a wacky motto: "A dry crack is a happy crack!" Mr. Happy Crack has his own line of apparel and his own website, but he's best known for generating business for The Crack Team. The company has a reputation for great work, but it wouldn't have grown to nationwide acclaim if it weren't for its word-of-mouth-worthy name.

Potbelly Sandwich Works didn't take itself too seriously when one of its Chicago stores was covered with construction scaffolding. Neighboring stores hung the usual cheap banners announcing they were still open. Potbelly took advantage of the opportunity and turned their banner into a word of mouth topic. Their sign: *Here Is a Potbelly Restaurant Disguised as a Construction Site.* How many people walked past that sign, told a coworker, and ordered some lunch?

Silly doesn't have to be complicated. For years, I've been publishing newsletters with names like "Damn, I Wish I'd Thought of That" and "You Can Be an Email Marketing Super-genius." These newsletters are good, but the names get them noticed and forwarded.

Partnering with a Charity

Partnering with a charity gives you an immediate topic. People tell their friends, "Buy from that store. It goes to a great cause." It's a genuine chance to do something good and a proven way to start positive word of mouth.

For each of my organization's conferences, we donate tickets to charity and auction them off. We sometimes get far more publicity and word of mouth from the auction than we do from the rest of our marketing. Similarly, many of the stores that sell stuff on eBay for you offer to waive their commissions for local churches that want to sell donated used goods to raise money. It doesn't cost the store much—and everyone in the church talks about it.

From a word of mouth perspective, charities are especially powerful because they come with their own built-in network of talkers. When you connect with any nonprofit, from a national organization to a single, small youth group, everyone in that group has a reason to talk about you. They are organized, involved, and have ready-to-go communication channels.

Think about the talkers when you pick a group to partner with. Donating to the Red Cross won't get you a lot of special attention. It's too common. An unusual cause or a local group may be much more excited about the relationship. You're well within the bounds of good taste if you ask a partner to send an announcement about your contribution.

STEP 2: CREATE A CAMPAIGN WORTH TALKING ABOUT

Your next best topics will come from campaigns that you launch specifically to generate word of mouth. These aren't as quick as the instant ideas above, but they aren't too hard, either. You can probably get most of these going in a few weeks.

Repeatable Advertising

Good advertising can be the topic of a word of mouth campaign. From Wendy's "Where's the Beef?" to Budweiser's "Whassup!" campaign, ads that stick in the mind start up the conversation.

Repeatable ads work because they get word of mouth. Word of mouth works when it's created by a repeatable ad.

We like to talk about advertising. In fact, a substantial amount of what we consider word of mouth about products is actually about the *advertising* for the products. You can't guarantee that an ad will be worth talking about, but it's worth trying.

You should try to build word of mouth into every advertising campaign.

Staples came up with a great ad campaign with a good motto: "That was easy." The ads featured an "Easy Button" that you could press to make life easier. They turned it into a word of mouth campaign—with impact far beyond the advertising— by selling toy Easy Buttons in their stores. They've sold more than a million buttons. People put them on their desks. It gets talked about in a million offices. (And they donated the sales from the buttons to charity.)

When you advertise, you are putting out a lot of cash to tell something to a large number of people. Wouldn't it be nice if those people repeated it?

Viral Campaigns

Viral campaigns are email messages specifically created to be forwarded to lots of people. The content can be anything: coupons, newsletters, or product updates. But they are usually some kind of game, joke, or funny video.

This technique is used so often that some people think that viral email is the same thing as word of mouth, but it's just one of many things that you can do.

There is no secret formula here. Hire a designer, create something fun, and send it out. Chances are, in between the few work-related messages you have, your inbox is crowded with forwarded stuff that your friends and coworkers think you will want to see. All that stuff is viral.

There's a lot of luck involved, and sometimes just good timing. You can create a great email, send it out, and it may get passed along instantly to millions of readers. Or it may go nowhere.

Viral emails may be kind of dumb, they may even be completely unrelated to the product, but they do get attention. Not all marketers are fans of this technique. Some think it's a little forced, with little genuine connection to the positive qualities of your brand. But when they work, they are huge successes.

The most reliable viral topic is a simple coupon. A few years ago, my interns started coming into the office all jittery and wired. I thought we had a drug problem.

We did. It was a coupon being sent around by email offering a free coffee at any Starbucks location inside a Barnes & Noble bookstore. There were lines out the door as the email was forwarded back and forth across the city. All the books and fancy lattes they sold were probably worth ten times the cost of the free coffee.

Free Information

Giving away free content is a great way to get people talking.

Give them market research, reports, white papers, webcasts, newsletters, anything. Free information provides rich, meaty topics that are perfect for starting word of mouth conversations. As you put more and more information out there, you feed deeper, more relevant discussions. Someone is much more likely to talk about new research that you have just given them than a one-off promotion.

Best of all, most of these items are portable, easy to share, and cheap to produce.

I created a series of simple articles for my last company and put them on the website as free downloads. These simple, one-page documents were each less than 500 words. More than 10,000 have been downloaded, and most have been passed along by email. Salesforce.com shares the video and text presentations from every conference that it has ever done. It is an incredibly valuable storehouse of content that makes its product that much more useful. It's also a constant conversation starter around the office. Book publishers take advantage of the opportunity to share the first chapter of a debut novel to create buzz and get people reading.

Without a doubt, the most powerful thing you can give away is a free weekly email newsletter. It's easy to produce, relevant to the reader, and easy to pass along. If you don't have an email newsletter, start one today.

Some people worry that giving away too much information might undercut the value of their products. It never happens. The stuff you share proves your expertise and attracts customers. It makes them want to talk *about* you and *to* you.

Wacky Stunts

Wienermobile: Generating word of mouth since 1936.

A high-profile stunt can create an instant topic that gets tons of word of mouth. It won't necessarily create deep, sophisticated conversations about your brand, but it will get you talked about.

Jones Soda doesn't have the resources to out-advertise Coke and Pepsi, but they know how to generate word of mouth. One Thanksgiving, they created a whole series of nasty, awful soda flavors, including Brussels Sprout with Prosciutto, Broccoli Casserole, and Smoked Salmon Paté.

Undrinkable. But talkable.

I'm sure we weren't the only family who had a taste test party. Anyone who saw these flavors is talking about them, and they are sure to notice the normal flavors next time they are at the store.

One of the wackiest stunts I've heard of is the story of Half.com the website and Half.com the town. Half.com was a marketplace website much like any other. In the dot-com boom, they needed attention like everyone else. What's a site to do? Well, they convinced a small town in Oregon (population 345) to change its name from Halfway to Half.com for a year. This first-of-its-kind coup landed Half.com on the map (literally) and generated substantial national publicity and gobs of word of mouth.

Yahoo! loves high-profile publicity stunts that get people talking. On their 10th birthday, they partnered with Baskin-Robbins to give a free ice cream cone to anyone who downloaded a coupon. Target showed up in Manhattan on a sweltering day with a truckload of $99 air conditioners. They didn't even have a store there, but everyone was talking about them. And there's the always-buzzworthy Nathan's hot-dog-eating contest.

A great stunt doesn't need to be expensive or complex. Just fun. Hold a contest. Host a party. Hire guys in Elvis suits. I saw an inflatable dinosaur and a robot hand in a store window. Not fancy, but kids were coming from all over the shopping mall to check it out, and they brought their parents.

STEP 3: BECOME A
BUZZWORTHY COMPANY

The best topic of all: Being a company worth talking about, all the way through.

Long-term, sustainable word of mouth comes when a business becomes truly immersed in the word of mouth philosophy. Your brand becomes fundamentally talkworthy as you reach inside your company and change how you think about business and your relationship with your customers.

These changes aren't easy, and sometimes they're radical. Not every company can make it happen. But your success is locked in if you can create a truly buzzworthy experience. You transform from a business that is constantly pushing out messages through expensive advertising to one that is pulling in customers, for free, through word of mouth.

Great Products

Extraordinary products create sustainable, long-term, company-changing word of mouth.

Create irresistible things, and people are guaranteed to talk forever. Unfortunately, there's no way to teach you *how* to do this. It must come from within.

Viking stoves. Moleskine notebooks. Corky's BBQ. Tiffany diamonds. Manolo Blahnik shoes. See's Candies. Peter Lugar's Steak House. The things that make you go *oooh*.

In all of these cases, the topic is clear: People love the stuff.

Uniqueness

"Did you know about _____?" is the start of so many word of mouth conversations. We like to share topics that are surprising, special, and one of a kind.

Be unique. Do things that are, by their nature, an interesting topic of conversation.

Try to create topics that only you can be associated with. This feels a bit like the classic marketing concept of *positioning*—owning a unique place in the customer's mind. In this case, you want to own a unique place in the customer's conversation.

Nike lets you order completely customized shoes, with your own style, color, decoration, and personalization. Anyone who owns these will be talking about them. And everyone who gets talked to will know that the shoes are Nike.

The Trader Joe's grocery chain has built a word of mouth empire on the power of unique products. The entire store is full of unusual house-brand items that are fantastic—and available nowhere else. They sell a bruschetta topping that my parents (who live in Florida) are nuts about. They make us mail it to them from Chicago. My dad tells his friends, who tell their children in Milwaukee. The last thing I heard, the daughter of a friend of a friend of my parents was trekking 90 miles to Chicago for a $3 condiment. Multiply by 300 products that you can't get anywhere else, and you have a sense of how powerful uniqueness can be.

Crayola's R&D geniuses invented magic markers that only work on special paper—and not on walls or children. This is so good, it practically speaks for itself. Every parent who tries them is on the phone immediately, telling every one of his or her friends.

A Shopping Experience

Do you want everyone who visits your store to become an instant talker? Make your entire store a topic. Turn the joint into a word of mouth experience.

People want to do more than shop. That's why the absurdly enormous Mall of America gets 42 million visitors each year.

Adventure outfitter REI lets you test climbing gear on in-store, three-story climbing walls and test shoes on simulated mountain trails. They teach classes on how to use their gadgets and how to master a variety of outdoor activities.

This works for local, small stores also.

Laura told Julie who told Andy who told Karen about . . . a dentist. The husband and wife team at Delaware Dental, in Chicago, have turned their practice into something special by creating a "dental lounge." The office is decorated in funky, modern colors. Instead of the pan-flute version of the Beatles' greatest hits, they ask about your musical taste on your patient information form. The topic: A unique atmosphere that makes a routine visit remarkable.

Take a look at how a bridal salon would create an experience. It's not just about the bride. Our talkers also are mom, little sister, best friend, and the bridesmaids. Give *them* an experience. Create a comfy place to hang out. Feed them well. Keep them entertained. The bride's gang will have far more word of mouth conversations than the bride herself.

Build It into Your Brand

Some companies are built from the ground up to work through word of mouth. The topics are obvious, because the reason to talk is the essence of their business plan.

There are a lot of ways to buy insurance on the internet. Progressive Insurance helps its customers by providing the price quotes from its competitors, even when the competitors' prices are better. That's a topic worth talking about. They built an entire company around a word of mouth concept, with no real risk, because buyers are checking prices anyway. The entire concept of the company is woven into the word of mouth topic.

Best Buy's computer repair service is perfect for word of mouth: It's called the Geek Squad. The staff wear nerdy uniforms. They drive special Geekmobiles that are usually parked on the sidewalk in front of the store where everyone can see them. Every bit of the concept makes you want to talk about it, even when you don't need computer repair. And you'll remember them when you do.

You can make a company word-of-mouth-ready by choosing customers who are also talkers. My parents once owned a one-hour photo lab. Their customers were random shoppers off the street, and were hard to reach without big advertising. So they sold it and opened a specialty photo lab that catered to professional photographers and advertising agencies. Those are communities of tightly connected talkers who know each other and talk to each other. It worked so well that they didn't even need a storefront with expensive rent—they moved into the fourth floor of a nondescript office building. People knew where they were through word of mouth.

The Demeter Fragrance Library isn't your regular collection of perfumes. If you really want to, they have perfumes that will make you smell like rye bread, tomato, or Play-Doh. Would anyone want to spray on a little lobster or earthworm? The word of mouth from the unusual scents got them the breakthrough they needed in a tough business—enough to get them stocked at major cosmetics counters.

You don't see many brands that are built for word of mouth. It's hard to do. It takes a top-to-bottom commitment to make it happen. But it's something to strive for.

Five Lessons from IKEA

You never forget your first trip to IKEA. Mine was in college. My roommate James initiated me into the cult. We drove 30 miles for some cheap furniture and a chance to see what all the talk was about. In the past 20 years, I have initiated dozens more people and probably brought IKEA tens of thousands of dollars in word of mouth sales.

A visit to IKEA is a fun day trip instead of the usual furniture-shopping hell. It's almost like going to Disneyland. Here are five word of mouth topics built into a single shopping experience.

1. *Surprising.* You always find some crazy, fun items that you never expected. Like a $15 turtle-shaped chair.

2. *Kid friendly.* Shopping for furniture with toddlers is a usually a recipe for disaster. IKEA makes it bearable, providing inexpensive diapers, baby food, and daycare services for parents who want some quality shopping time. Can you imagine letting Kmart babysit for you?

3. *Tasty.* I go just for the Swedish meatballs. The restaurant is so good (and cheap) that lunch is a highlight.

4. *Mystery.* Every product name is Swedish. The names are so quirky that there are websites dedicated to decoding them. Need a Jerker, a Skänka, or some Skydd?

5. *Good products.* You know what you're getting when you buy from IKEA. Cool, cheap stuff. It's pretty much a sure thing. It's worth your time, and worth telling your friends about.

CHAPTER SIX

Tools: How Can You Help the Message Travel?

YOUR JOB: MAKE IT EASIER FOR THE MESSAGE TO SPREAD

Word of mouth is powerful, but it doesn't go on forever. When people talk to each other, the conversation only travels a short distance.

Word of mouth gets much, much more powerful when you help it along.

It's nice when someone tells a friend about you—it's nicer when they post an online review that everyone sees. It's nice when someone shares a coupon that you give them—it's nicer when they email that coupon to 50 friends.

Once you've identified your talkers and have a topic you want them to talk about, it's time to figure out everything you can do to accelerate the process. The tools we discuss here are some of the many things you can use to help get the message out.

Remember our original definition: Giving people a reason to talk about your stuff and *making it easier for the conversation to take place*. That's what the tools are all about.

LEGO discovered something interesting: Grownups like to play with LEGOs, too. It was a relatively quiet, inactive group, until LEGO put up a message board where all those people could get together, talk about their hobby, and share ideas. As you can imagine, word of mouth took off like crazy. The tool was a message board that supercharged an existing, low-level conversation. The community became active, involved, and connected—and it turns out that adults have a lot more money to spend than toddlers.

Tools don't have to be complicated. One of the lost word of mouth classics is the free postcards that used to be in every hotel room. A postcard is just a little advertisement for your hotel. Sending that postcard home used to be a ritual. It was a great tool, a simple way to make it easier for people to tell their friends. A postcard is word of mouth perfection.

Fast-Moving Waters

The key concepts to keep in mind with tools are *speed* and *portability*.

Think of your topic as a drop of oil on a fast-moving river. The moment it touches the surface, it spreads far and wide in a high-speed rush. Things like viral emails, popular blogs, and product reviews sites are examples of major currents that you want to ride. These are the tools that drive accelerated word of mouth today.

Here's a simple suggestion: Put your latest topic in the bottom of all your outgoing emails. Do it for the whole company. You might send 50 to 500 emails each week. Your entire office sends many times more—and always to people who are actively engaged with your company. Think of your email signature as an idea-insertion vehicle. Change the message once a month and you have a powerful tool to get portable topics moving.

The Internet Is Your Most Powerful Tool

Much of this section will talk about how to use the internet to accelerate word of mouth. The most efficient and effective tools are online. As I've pointed out, 80 percent of word of mouth happens offline, and you should focus on the talkers, topics, and taking part that occur in the real world. But when it comes to spreading your messages faster and farther, the internet is the communications engine. Just remember that online tools spark conversations that may begin on the internet but don't necessarily end there.

THREE MUST-USE WORD OF MOUTH MARKETING TOOLS

Grab a pencil. Write this down.

If you do nothing else I recommend, if you ignore the rest of this book, put these three things on your to-do list. They will get you more word of mouth than anything:

The Three Must-Use Word of Mouth Marketing Tools

1. Ask people to spread the word

2. Put everything in an email

3. Put a tell-a-friend link on every page of your website

These tools are free, they are easy, and they are the most effective ways to turn a single recommendation into powerful word of mouth.

Ask People to Spread the Word

Sometimes, all you need to do is ask.

The first and foremost tool for creating word of mouth is the easiest and most obvious: asking nicely. Most people won't talk until you ask them to. So ask often and ask everywhere.

The challenge isn't necessarily finding talkers; it's triggering the talking action. Often, the implied compliment of asking customers to help is what starts them down the road to becoming talkers. Remember that inviting your talkers to spread the word is a way of conferring status and making them insiders.

The term for this is a "call to action." These are visual and verbal requests for people to do something. Weave calls to action into everything you do. Use the power of suggestion. It works. Here are some ideas:

- Put the words "Tell a friend," "Pass it on," or something like that all over your website. (It doesn't matter if they click on them. The visual reminder puts the idea in their heads.)

- Put these words in every email, too.

- Train your sales staff to end each sale with a thank you and a friendly, "Don't forget to tell your friends."

- Put a request on the receipt.

- Put a sign on the door.

- Send a reminder email after each online order.

Before my organization's annual conference, we sent a message to every one of our members, asking them to email their clients and associates about the conference. We also asked them to post a reminder to their blogs and newsletters. Each recipient was given a unique "secret" discount code, which made them look good when they passed it along. The codes were fun, which encouraged sharing. (Company XYZ's secret code was "weloveXYZ.")

Volunteers need to be asked to volunteer. Most people won't step up on their own. Nonprofit organizations are used to doing this. So are missionary churches. They know that raising money or getting converts is the second step, after asking a bunch of talkers to go out and spread the word.

Asking is easy. But most companies forget to do it.

Put It in an Email

Put it in an email. Put it in an email. Put *everything* in an email.

Email is the fastest, most portable, most effective word of mouth tool ever invented. Email is freedom for ideas to move.

By definition, when you put a topic in an email, you are making it viral. Take everything you are doing and email it to someone. Create an email newsletter so you can send topics to lots of people. Let talkers sign up for your email lists on your home page.

A coupon is a single-user promotion. An email coupon can bring in thousands of new people through word of mouth.

If you really want an email to take off, use these essential strategies for high-velocity email:

- *Make sure it's forwardable.* Far too many overdesigned emails fall apart when forwarded, with broken graphics and links. Send it to yourself, on different accounts and computers, and make sure it looks great when passed along.

- *Write it for the second recipient.* Make sure that your email makes sense to pass-along readers who get it from a friend. They may not know who you are. Add sections for "About the Company," "About This Newsletter," and anything else that tells your exciting story to someone who is seeing you for the first time.

- *Capture new talkers.* Every email should have sign-up instructions right in the message. Don't expect secondhand recipients to go to your site and search for how to get on the list. Grab them while they are hot and ready to act.

- *Tell recipients to tell a friend.* Put a big, bold call to action right at the top. Remember, talkers talk when you ask them to. Include a link to a tell-a-friend form right in the message.

These great email tricks are also worth a try.

- *Be funny.* Put something amusing at the end of every message just to get it forwarded. The last story of my newsletter is always funny, often weird, and rarely related to the rest of the message. People love to pass along odd stuff, so the fun bit causes the forwarding, and the marketing messages go along for the ride.

- *Tell readers NOT to forward the message.* Works every time. My most-forwarded messages all start with the phrase "PRIVATE: DO NOT FORWARD."

Tell-a-Friend Forms

Put a tell-a-friend form or link on every page of your website.

It can be a little icon or link that says "tell a friend" or "email this page" or whatever. You can get fancy and add a little form right on the page for people to fill out.

Think about it. Someone is on your website, looking at something that you are selling—and they feel the urge to tell someone else. *Make it easy.* That person is about to advertise for you, for free. Or they need to ask someone a question before they buy. Or they just like what they see. Do whatever it takes to let that word of mouth happen.

A desire to make a referral is a magic moment. Make sure the magic is only one click away. Plus, it reinforces the "just ask" principle.

Don't let your webmaster get in the way or tell you that this is too complicated or expensive. You can have this installed on your site in less than one hour, for less than $100. (I've been using a great little tool called Master Recommend Pro from Willmaster.com for almost 10 years, on dozens of sites. It costs $49.)

Here are the secrets to creating effective referral forms:

- *Make it fast.* Design a form that can be filled out in less than 15 seconds. Get rid of optional fields, passwords, or anything that gets in the way of the referral.

- *Ask for several referrals.* Be sure to explicitly ask users to forward the message to multiple friends. The more you ask, the more you get. Design the form so it is easy to add lots of names without confusion.

- *Use the sender's name.* When you deliver the message, make sure it is from the referrer, not your website. The recipient isn't expecting mail from you and might delete it. He will open a message from his friend.

- *Include a personal message.* Let the sender add text to the message. The referral is far more powerful when the talker gets to put it in his own words.

- *Make it reforwardable.* Take a look at the message that recipients get. Is that message a ready-to-go viral email, or is it some cryptic link? Follow the advice above for creating a good viral email.

- *Protect privacy.* And brag about it. Be clear and explicit that you respect the privacy of the senders and recipients using the form and that you won't use their emails for any other purpose (and stick to what you promise). Usage will skyrocket when you do this.

MULTIPLY THE SHARING

It's a shame if a talker only talks to one person.

Expand the power of your talkers by making it easier for them to share with more than one person at a time. Add extra lines for more recipients on your tell-a-friend forms. Be sure that your talkers have all the brochures and freebies they want. Always ask for two referrals instead of one. Don't send one copy of your book or product to review—send enough for the entire office. That will get everyone to try it and to talk about it.

When Seth Godin published a compilation of essays called *The Big Moo*, he primed the pump before its official publication date by offering prerelease copies for $2 each. But the catch was, you had to buy a case of 50. He made the offer to people he knew would talk up the book and pass it along to other interested talkers. The proceeds from this prepublication sale went to charity, and Godin put 10,000 copies of the book in the hands of 200 of his best talkers.

Twofers

The classic "two for the price of one" offer is all about word of mouth. This works best with things that need a second person present, like a movie ticket (it's hard to sit in two seats at the same time). You get bonus word of mouth when the talker is asking around, looking for that friend to share it with.

Costco sometimes offers a free membership for a friend when a current member renews. It's a great idea. The current member gets the status of setting up her friend with a great deal, and she spreads word of mouth while she is looking for someone to give it to. Costco makes up the cost on the renewal of the friend the next year (and then she brings a friend, too.)

The Week magazine sent me a subscription card that offered a free subscription for a friend if we signed up at the same time. I'd been meaning to subscribe, so the offer gave me the impetus I needed to do it, plus a real reason to talk about *The Week* to my friends. I talked to four people in the office before one took the freebie. The magazine got good word of mouth and at least two new subscribers.

Make Your Pages Super-Viral

Make it really, really easy for users to share your web pages. You can do so much more than just the standard tell-a-friend form. Design the entire page to encourage word of mouth.

YouTube is a website where anyone can upload homemade videos and share them with friends. In 2006, the site came from nowhere to become far bigger than competing services from well-funded giants Yahoo! and Google.

Its secret? It is really good at asking people to email their friends, and makes it incredibly easy. Look at how many ways YouTube makes it easy for you to share:

- Every page has a "Share Video" link.
- Every page has the HTML code ready to paste right into your own website.
- Every page has a "Blog Video" link that can automatically add the video to your blog without taking you away from YouTube.
- After you watch the video, it replaces the show with another "Share This Video" link.
- It provides a super-simple form for sharing that takes less than three seconds to use.
- It saves the emails of people you send to, so you can send to them again. This is powerful. If you send a video to

your mom the first time, and your sister the second time, both email addresses are waiting to be used again without retyping. The next time you go to share a video with your dad, there's good chance that you'll also send it to mom and sis, because their emails are right there.

Build Word of Mouth into Your Product

Look for ways to build word of mouth right into your stuff. The challenge: Add qualities or features that make spreading the word an automatic result of using the product.

The creation of Hotmail is a classic story of word of mouth marketing. In 18 months, the company went from zero to more than eight million users, then was sold for $400 million, with little more promotion than word of mouth. The secret? Every email had a little link at the bottom that said "Get Your Free Email from Hotmail." Hotmail is what we would call a pure viral product—there is no way to use the product without also spreading word of mouth about it.

For a generation, what was the first thing you did with a Polaroid photo? You gave it to a friend. Polaroid made its stuff even more portable when it came up with film that was sticky on the back. Photos so ready to travel that you can stick them to people, bikes, and cars.

It won't work for everything, but try to find features that make using your product and sharing your product part of the same process.

Look for Network Effects

If you had the only fax machine in the world, it would be useless. If a few people have them it's okay, but they get exponentially more useful as more people get them. That's the network effect. You've seen it for phones, faxes, email, instant messaging, and most new communication technologies. Network effects put out giant waves of word of mouth.

The latest example of this is Skype, an internet-only phone service that is mostly used for calling other Skype users. You need your friends to have an account if you want to call them with it, so you bug them and talk about its benefits. Other internet phone services don't have the same power of network-effect word of mouth, because their phones make calls to regular phone lines. There's no reason to talk to your friends about it, because it doesn't matter to you whether they use it or not.

Think about calling circles, buddy lists, team discounts, and any other reason why a customer would benefit when her friends use your product, too.

STUFF TO SHARE

Don't expect anyone to remember to talk about you. Put something in their hands that reminds them, motivates them, and makes them look good.

Give them stuff to share.

Electronic Pass-Alongs

Create an entire package of electronic cut-and-paste pass-alongs. Include everything talkers might need if they were going to post something about you on the internet. At a minimum, you need:

- Logos, banner ads, and icons. Make them in all the standard sizes so they will fit wherever someone wants to paste them.
- Sample text in different styles and lengths.
- Ready-to-forward email messages.

You get even more word of mouth when you create richer content. More interesting items are more likely to get forwarded. Try sounds, animations, ecards, and cut-and-paste code that inserts the promotion right into web pages.

The more you give to your talkers, the easier it is for them to talk. Just as important, you gain a little bit of control over the content and look of the message when you give them the words and images.

When announcing a new project, create a special email that asks your talkers to help you spread the word. The top of the message should have an introduction and explanation, along with some ready-to-paste images and sample text. The bottom of the message should be a ready-to-forward email promotion, already mail-merged with the talker's name. All they need to do is trim off the top and forward it.

Handouts and Takeaways

Never let somebody walk out of your store empty-handed.

Remember when smokers roamed free in restaurants, bars, and other public places? Every restaurant gave away matchbooks with its logo on the cover. They were a useful little takeaway that reminded the customer of the business every time he lit up—and they were passed along. Well, with smoking on the decline, what replaces the matchbook? Think of little doodads your customers could pick up and use. Then slap your name and your topic all over them.

Give the shopper something to stuff in her pocket and show to a friend, a spouse, a coworker. Pens, calendars, and magnets are some of the many things you can hand out for free to keep the conversation going. At the very least, have business cards or pocket-sized flyers by the cash register.

These handouts have two simple functions. They remind the talker to talk (when they get taken out of the pocket or shopping bag later), and they give talkers something to talk about.

They are conversation starters.

If you sell expensive or complicated products, put little info flyers next to each item on display. A sheet of paper with product specifications is also a tool that a shopper can take home and show someone. It helps the shopper make a purchase decision—but it also allows the product and store to get talked about more easily to someone new.

I'm boggled by executives who make public speeches but don't take the time to bring any sort of handout. It doesn't matter what you bring, but think about the huge multiplier effect when the audience goes back to the office and shares your handout with lots of coworkers.

Think about that simple thing you can hand to your talkers to remind them to talk.

Stuff the Package

If your company sells products via catalog or the web, you don't have face-to-face contact with your customers, and your customers don't rub elbows in your store.

How do you turn those buyers into talkers?

You stuff the box with word of mouth tools.

The package that you ship is a great word of mouth opportunity—and you can put plenty in there without adding any postage expense. Think of all the cool stuff you could throw in that might get your customers talking about you.

At the very least, put the following in every package that you ship: three coupons to share with friends, three catalogs or flyers, and three samples of something. Put the tools to make a referral right in the customer's hands. It's a great time to do it. They are excited about having just received their new product, and they are probably primed to become talkers.

Even better, surprise them with something fun. A handwritten thank-you will blow them away. Include a nice case for the product. When I buy laminating supplies by mail, I find a bag of M&Ms in every order. It's just unusual enough that I tell people about it, and the office interns tell their friends at other companies (after stealing my candy).

Honeymoon Kit

Remember those brand-new customers who may be your most prolific (but short-term) talkers? You need a fast-acting tool to turn them on before they fade away.

Capture that new-customer enthusiasm during the honeymoon period by creating a honeymoon kit that gives them everything they need to start talking. Fill it with the same pass-along items mentioned above. Hand them an envelope with a welcome letter and some coupons to share.

Every customer who buys from Dale and Thomas Popcorn can immediately send a free sample to anyone else. New customers are talking before their order even ships.

For more complex products, you can create an entire welcome experience. Include training materials, a disk of logos to put on the recipient's web site, useful documents, and some fun items, too. Include a survey that asks for the names of other people you should be talking to in their company.

Go ahead and ask your new customer to give you a referral. Someone who just made a decision to do business with you will want to reinforce that decision by getting their friends involved. Plus, you flatter them and make them feel included in your family when you ask for help.

Build It to Be Stolen

Market research company eMarketer is a master of the concept of cut-and-paste word of mouth. Their email newsletters and website are full of fantastic graphs and charts. Each image is perfectly sized to paste right into a report or Power-Point. It also is designed so you can't help but see that it's from eMarketer.

The word of mouth power of this technique is amazing. Every day, executives across the country are showing off eMarketer in meetings, speeches, and memos. Massive word of mouth. eMarketer keeps it going with fresh new topics (ready-to-copy charts) every week. Why advertise when people will show you off for free?

What can you do to make your stuff easier to steal and share?

Samples and Seeding

Here's something so obvious that most people miss it: People don't talk about things that they have never seen or tried. (Okay, some people do, but who listens to them?)

You need to get samples of your products into your talkers' hands to kick off the conversation.

The legend of the launch of Post-it Notes is a wonderful word of mouth story. At first, the product was going nowhere, because nobody had seen these things or knew what to do with them (or even to ask for them). So the secretary of the CEO of 3M started using them on documents sent to executives around the country, and sent samples to the secretaries of other Fortune 500 CEOs. Needless to say, they used them, they shared them, and the rest is history. (Post-its have great built-in word of mouth qualities, because you usually share them when you use them.)

There's nothing new about the idea of free samples. Marketers have been using them forever. But there is a specific word of mouth marketing application of the technique. The goal is to get samples into the hands of the most likely talkers. It's not about giving stuff away to potential customers; it's about getting the product in the hands of potential word of mouth advocates. The term that's often used for this is *seeding*—you are planting the seed of a conversation.

If you've got a good list of talkers, you can mail them something. You can also keep samples handy for those especially chatty customers when they come into the store. When Coca-Cola launched Coke Zero, they sent a case home with every employee. That's a lot of free samples and a lot of conversations.

The trick is to know where your talkers are. Public venues tend to attract connected talkers—concerts, sporting events, bars, and any place social people gather. It may be a mass event like a baseball game, or it may be a small but influential business function.

Trade shows are a great place to reach highly concentrated talker groups. Your sample doesn't need to match the theme of the event—it just needs to be something that these folks will take home to show their friends.

Tylenol has a fantastic program in which they sponsor skateboarding competitions. They know that the participants are highly social, very connected talkers. And these kids seriously need painkillers. These talkers are also very resistant to advertising and would probably turn against marketers who blatantly try to sell to them. So Tylenol does something very clever: It pays to support the events, but it doesn't put up any signs or logos. It just provides free painkillers and lets the word spread naturally. The company knows that it has found the right talkers—and those talkers know who's providing the cash. The gratitude spreads through word of mouth.

The Power of Swag

Never underestimate the power of swag—free hats, shirts, bags, toys, or anything with company logos on it.

While it's true there is a guy somewhere who will sell you advertising space on his forehead, most of us will never find anyone who would accept any amount of money to be a human billboard. Yet people will display your logo every day on a hat or shirt.

If people identify with your brand and love your stuff, wearing or carrying your logo around is a way to support you. Sometimes it's unintentional. I've been carrying around a PayPal backpack for an entire year. (It's a nice bag.) I don't use PayPal often, but I've been displaying the company's logo at every speech I deliver, in front of hundreds of people.

Every item with your logo becomes a word of mouth generator when it's worn by a real person. It starts conversations and gets people asking about it. And precisely because it's not paid advertising but a personal expression, the message is authentic and credible, a recommendation instead of a commercial.

So give away lots of free stuff.

Conversation Starters

Create simple items that prompt a word of mouth conversation. Many talkers won't start a conversation about you but will sing your praises if anyone else mentions you. So do things that get you mentioned.

I've taken every business card that I've received in the past ten years, glued my logo to the back, used a laminator to turn it into a luggage tag, and mailed it back to the person I just met. There are probably 10,000 people with my logo on their briefcase or suitcase. When they meet each other, they talk about my company. That's a lot of word of mouth.

A great organization called the Association Forum was recruiting new members. Membership in an association isn't one of those things that just pops up in everyday conversations. So they made bobblehead dolls to send to their current members, who were thrilled to get the cool toy. Next time a coworker noticed the doll sitting on a member's desk, it prompted an instant word of mouth conversation. Sales jumped.

BLOGS

In the context of word of mouth marketing, here's why blogs matter: They are a tool for extending and accelerating the conversation. Starting one is a long-term commitment, but it's not hard to do. The payoff is worth it.

This section isn't about how to blog. There are plenty of books about that. This is about how blogs create word of mouth.

Blogs Make Messages Portable

Blogs are all about linking, sharing, and connecting.

Put a topic on a blog, and it's instantly ready for word of mouth. Every blog post has instructions for how to link to it and how to email it, and provides credit and recognition for those who do.

This is why they have been so successful: A story on a blog gets picked up by other blogs, and visitors get linked back and forth between them. In the same way emails spread virally, the way blogs link to each other helps websites spread. On top of that, blog entries show up very prominently in search engines.

Blogs Create New Topics

Your company probably has a lot to say and a lot to share. But you can't issue a press release every day.

A blog is the tool that lets you put out fresh ideas and information. It is designed for small, frequent updates—almost like having your own news wire. It's the perfect way to keep your talkers fed with new topics and ideas. Everything you post gives people something new to talk about.

Blogs Provide a Place for the Conversation to Happen

Talkers need other people to talk to. A blog becomes the location of that conversation. It brings everyone together, it connects the conversation to similar ones on other blogs, and it provides a place to go when someone wants to talk. The blog provides critical mass that takes conversations to the next level.

Just look at the comments on a blog. All those little responses represent talkers who wanted to express their opinions. The blog makes it possible, and it is the tool that shares that conversation with other readers.

Blogging Builds Credibility

Bloggers respect bloggers. You can't just show up and expect everyone to talk about you, any more than you can show up at a party and expect to be the center of attention. You've gotta earn it.

Sooner or later, you're going to want to be blogged about, or you're going to need to respond to a negative blog comment. When that happens, you don't want to be a stranger.

Start blogging now, so you have time to build relationships and credibility before you need it. You want to become a known quantity and a part of the conversation. That way, when you are ready to interact with blogs, you are seen as a member of the community instead of a crass marketer looking for shameless publicity.

ONLINE COMMUNITIES AND
SOCIAL MEDIA

With all the attention that blogs are getting, it's easy to forget that there is a far bigger, older world of message boards and online communities. These are the high-energy homes of word of mouth. Discussions about products and services start, spread, and stay there permanently.

These are powerful tools that you need to learn to work with.

It doesn't matter what you are selling. Someone has created an online community for your industry. These forums are active and very focused, sometimes focused on exactly what you do.

I was shopping for picture frames online and found dozens of stores that carried pretty much the same thing. But it only took one glowing review on a message board for photographers about a particular store's reliable shipping to make my decision. I trusted the genuine word of mouth from someone I'd never met. And I found it in a place no traditional marketer would consider relevant.

Your customers are doing the same research about you.

Create Your Own Message Board

Message boards are easy to install, are usually free, and create an instant home for your talkers. Put one on your site, and you'll find all sorts of talkers coming out of the woodwork to participate. When they do, the board creates a public word of mouth archive to attract future discussions.

We've already discussed what LEGO and Intuit have done. It works just as well for small businesses. MusicToyz.com is a web store for guitar junkies. It's a one-man operation that could never afford a traditional advertising campaign. But its online forum is the best place to talk about eclectic, electric guitar gear.

The last time I looked, it had 3,500 registered users, 65 people online at once, and more than 200,000 messages posted. All that action is a written record of the word of mouth conversation. It grabs shoppers off the search engines and funnels them right into the store.

The New Hyperspeed Communities

"Social networks" are the latest type of online community to join the party. Sites like MySpace, LinkedIn, and Facebook are basically supercharged message boards that also have instant linking between users. Tens of millions of people have created a page on a social network, and word of mouth travels fast and furious between them.

Also important are the "social media" sites, where stories are added and edited entirely by consumers. Wikipedia is the global consumer-written encyclopedia, Digg is created by consumers linking their pages to a central library, Craigslist is the ultimate bulletin board, Flickr is full of uploaded photos, and YouTube is the home for everyone's videos.

Some think that these consumer-created content sites are a passing fad, but I doubt it. Those mentioned above were all among the hundred biggest websites as of June 2006. This is where people are talking to each other.

These sites are hotbeds of word of mouth. Much of the everyday conversation about products and services has moved to there, where it has been linked to, connected, and accelerated. It's too big too ignore.

Turning Social Sites into Word of Mouth Tools

No word of mouth tool has as much potential for scale and reach as the social networks and social media sites. You've hit

the big time if you can get your stuff picked up in the conversation stream. It's just a matter of getting involved. And, of course,
doing it ethically. I won't repeat the honesty rules here, but pay
close attention to them.

The good news is that participation is open, easy, and free.

Create Profiles and Pages. All of the social sites let you
set up your own account, with your own pages, identities, and
topics of conversation. Do this on any site where your customers
might be participating. Once you have a page, you have something for fans and friends to link to. Having a presence causes
the conversation to happen.

Each site has its own audience with a different style of com-
municating, and each one spreads word of mouth to a different
audience. Learn how each one works and then get in there.
This is a great job for an eager intern.

MySpace is so powerful that it is now essential for any new
band to create a page there before they do any other marketing.
Within minutes, they have an instant fan club. People hear
about the music, they link to it, and then share those links with
friends: instant viral word of mouth. But it's not just for teenagers and rock bands. There are pages for real estate agents,
investment bankers, radio DJs, Axe deodorant, and everything
else you can think of.

Be Social-Media Friendly. Many of the connections
and links on social media websites are automated. If you create
your pages the right way, you'll get included in the linking.
Most of the new sites use something called "tags," which are little bits of text that identify your web pages. Learn to tag,
because it will instantly connect your pages to the word of
mouth conversation. (This is an important tool, but too complicated to explain in this book. Do a little research—it's a
huge, free word of mouth opportunity.)

Ask Your Talkers to Connect to You. You can be sure that a significant number of your talkers are already participating in these communities and social networks. In fact, it is probably where they are already doing some of their talking about you. Don't sit back and hope to get noticed. Your success on these sites is a function of how many connections you have, so reach out to your talkers, tell them that you're there, and ask them to connect their pages to yours.

EXCLUSIVITY, SECRETS, AND SURPRISES

Exclusivity and participation are powerful word of mouth tools. They turn mildly interested people into rabid fans.

When you engage people in a product and make them feel as though it is *their* product, it translates directly into a desire to talk about it. Groupies are promoters—and all they want is a taste of what it's like to be the rock star. Look for ways to put specialness, exclusivity, and fun into being a talker.

Remember the Pepsi Challenge? Coke drinkers who chose Pepsi were surprised, Pepsi drinkers were self-congratulatory—and everyone was spreading word of mouth about Pepsi.

Make It Exclusive

Deep down inside, we all like to feel special. It's a strong motivator for word of mouth conversations. Many people are more likely to talk about a product if they have some kind of insider access or privileged status.

This is one of the reasons that the talker programs we discussed earlier work so well. When you call someone an ambassador, a VIP, or a member of the club, you're making them feel special. Every time they tell someone about your stuff, they are also reinforcing their status.

It works with any kind of status. When Google launched Gmail, its free email service, it made the product entirely word of mouth driven. In fact, the company made it a privilege to be allowed to share the product. The only way to get an account was if a friend invited you. First, you would receive an invitation from a friend (you feel special!). Once you were signed up, you got a limited number of invitations to send to your friends (now you're important!). In fact, after more than two years, you still can't sign up for the service unless you get a referral from a friend. What a great way to lock in the exclusivity topic.

Keep It Secret

It's human nature to want to share a secret. You should use the power of gossip to encourage word of mouth.

Instead of announcing your topics to your talkers—try hiding them. Make people work to dig them up. The fun of the hunt and the excitement of discovery are worth talking about. When talkers discover the secret benefit, they are that much more likely to want to blab the secret to everyone they know.

Restaurants can offer a special that only insiders know about. Have the waiter casually mention it to each new customer, on the sly. I bet they'll go right out and spread a little word of mouth about the delicious secret that they discovered. Some restaurants have set up a private phone number so regular customers can always get a reservation.

Stores can offer a product or add-on that isn't apparent to regular shoppers. Maybe special gift wrapping, a unique flavor, or a delivery service. Let the word spread that you have this available for people who ask.

Video games and DVDs have used this trick for years. They are full of what are called "Easter eggs," which are fun displays that are only revealed if you know the secret code. Conversation about where to find these surprises fills message boards and keeps people talking about the product.

Give Sneak Previews

Everyone wants to be a movie reviewer and get invited to exciting premieres. We like to see things first. Why? Because we feel special when we tell our friends.

The sneak preview is one of the most reliable word of mouth tools. The desire to get a preview is directly tied to the desire to talk about what you just saw.

Think of talkers as your advance team. Always give them an early taste of your next new thing. They will pay you back by talking to everyone and building demand before the product is even available. Give them an advanced look to keep them excited and enough information to look smart to the people they're talking to.

Keep it simple. Create an email list for insiders with upcoming offers and developments.

Retailers: Offer private shopping hours for your talkers the night before new products are available to the public. Restaurants: Host a preview meal to show off your new menu or chef. Car dealers: Invite your talkers in for a test drive of new cars before anyone even knows that they have arrived. Software companies: Send prerelease versions of software to anyone active on a related message board.

Cell phone companies have started sending new models not just to the big electronics publications but to hundreds of bloggers. That's a radical change. New models used to be top secret, with the manufacturers suing anyone who leaked the design. Now, leaks are a word of mouth motivator. (You should send out tester versions of new products to your fans, too.)

Let Your Talkers Build the Product

Talkers who get to see an early version of a product are usually eager to talk about it. When you let them participate, they become committed to the success and locked in as part of the team.

Google has dozens of new products in development—and you can play with every one of them right at Google Labs (*labs.google.com*). Anyone can try a product in development, suggest features, and discuss it online. That early participation guarantees that all sorts of people are aware of the product, involved, and ready to spread word of mouth when it launches.

The software industry has turned beta tests into immense word of mouth programs. Originally, beta tests were designed to get real users to debug products. These days, the programs are so huge, the word of mouth function is just as important. More than 300,000 people are testing the next version of Windows. Each one of those testers is now an insider, with a commitment to the success of the platform. People rarely criticize a product that they helped build.

TESTIMONIALS AND CUSTOMER REVIEWS

Word of mouth is so effective because of the natural credibility that comes from real people with no profit or agenda tied to their recommendations. It's those "people like us" whom we look for and listen to.

Recommendations, testimonials, and thank-you letters from those real people are great, but they are often invisible to potential customers. A testimonial sent to you in a private letter or email never reaches anyone else.

You've got a talker and you've got a topic. Now you need a tool, because the recommendation won't get to a new reader without your help.

Promote Positive Testimonials

Testimonials are nice to receive. But they have a much greater impact when you actively manage them. Don't just pile up that good feedback in a desk drawer—turn it into a word of mouth tool. The steps are simple:

1. *Ask for testimonials.* Most customers are glad to give them. But they won't think to do it without a little prompting. It is perfectly fine to ask any customer, "Would you mind giving me a short recommendation?" You should also have a form on your website where anyone can submit feedback of any sort. If the customer isn't sure what to say, feel free to suggest something. Just be careful not to cross the line by asking him to say something that he doesn't believe (the Honesty of Opinion rule applies here).

2. *Get permission to share.* Don't forget to ask for permission to use the testimonial in your marketing material. It will be very embarrassing if you use a testimonial and the recommender later denies having made it or has left her job. You'll need the written record to prove to that you had permission to mention the person and the company.

You don't need a formal contract, but do get an explicit okay in writing or in email. The easiest thing to do is add a check box to a form on the website. When someone sends you a nice email or an unsolicited compliment, you should also feel free to email them back for permission. I frequently send a note that says something like, "Thanks for the kind words. May I quote you in our marketing materials?"

3. *Put it all on your website.* This is the point! Show off all those kind recommendations. Put the word of mouth out there where everyone will see it.

4. *Link to compliments already on the web.* Now that you've got a page full of positive word of mouth, go surfing for anything else online. You'll find a ton on the blogs. Link to each of these. As long as it's posted publicly, you don't need explicit permission.

Work with Customer Review Sites

You obviously want to get good reviews wherever your products are discussed.

But you also need a large number of reviews.

When people scan the reviews for your stuff, they are looking for two things: First: Are the reviews good? Second: How many people have bothered to review you?

There's power in numbers. The quantity of reviews is a measure of how word-of-mouth-worthy your stuff is. If people are reviewing your products—good, bad, or mixed—you have a conversation you can work with. If no one is reviewing your products, it signals to the shopper that your stuff isn't even worth considering. Nobody is excited about it one way or the other. In the absence of reviews, many shoppers will assume the worst and look for a more popular product.

Sometimes you have to ask people to post reviews. Or do what eBay and others have done: Build a request for a review into the shopping transaction. Try putting a slip of paper into the box you ship. When you send an email receipt, include a link to the major sites that review you.

And remember—no padding the reviews and no employees logging in under fake names. Always be honest.

Capture Passive Word of Mouth

What is a best-seller list? It is passive word of mouth.

Each of those rankings represents an implicit recommendation made by a previous buyer. Those thousands of buyers may not have intentionally planned on engaging in word of mouth, but their collective voice is a powerful form of it.

There are other examples of this. Amazon's "Customers who bought this item also bought . . ." lists give you the implied recommendations of all those shoppers. iTunes lets you see other people's song lists. My personal favorite is the list of "most emailed stories" from newspapers' websites. It gives you a direct, explicit sense of what people are recommending.

When you tell your customer that "other people bought this," you are turning these passive recommendations into useful word of mouth. When you post your company's best-seller list, you give shoppers an instant sense of what other people are recommending and the confidence to choose based on those recommendations.

Put these lists on your website. Most online shopping carts already have modules for both a "most popular items" list and a "what other customers bought" list. If you're offline, put up a sign or a chalkboard with "Hot Products" or "Customer Favorites."

Don't make it complicated. In bookstores and video stores, the "Staff Favorites" shelf delivers word of mouth from the employees. Add another shelf for customer favorites.

CHAPTER SEVEN

Taking Part: How Can You Join the Conversation?

YOUR JOB: PARTICIPATE IN THE CONVERSATION

Most of us don't talk to ourselves. It's just not very interesting. We need someone else to hold up the other end of the conversation to keep it going.

Word of mouth is a dialog. Someone says something about you, and you answer. If you don't, it rarely goes any further. Your job is to jump in, be part of the conversation, and make it come alive. As you know by now, people are talking about you. Wouldn't you rather have them talking with you?

This is so easy to do that you'd be crazy not to do it. Anyone in your company who's interested can step up right now and start participating. Some can listen, some can respond, and some can be out there just monitoring the conversation.

This whole idea is not always easy for traditional marketers (especially spreadsheet-driven number lovers).

Marketing is fundamentally an outbound function: Think of an idea, blast it out there, and hope someone shows up. Most marketing departments aren't organized to accept input from customers or to engage in conversations with them. That's usually customer service's job. Customer service talks to people all day long and, hopefully, tries to make them happy. But customer service is rarely focused on making new sales, and, unfortunately, the average customer service department just wants to get people off the phone as quickly as possible. Marketing and customer service have to learn to work together if word of mouth is going to work for you.

> **Big Idea: Word of mouth is as much about customer service as it is about marketing.**

If you want good word of mouth, you'll have to participate. You have to be ready to talk to whomever wants to talk, about whatever they want to talk about.

There are two big risks to ignoring the conversation: Word of mouth dies, or word of mouth goes negative. These days, you stand a serious risk of word of mouth backlash if you aren't talking with customers when they are talking about you, and you have a greater risk of causing negative word of mouth if you're seen as out of it or snobby.

On the other hand, the more you encourage and participate in word of mouth, the more word of mouth you get. The upside is a valuable, energized, enthusiastic discussion with thousands of talkers who are bringing you loads of free business.

It's an easy decision. Get started!

HOW TO JOIN THE CONVERSATION

Remember this: People want you to participate, as long as you do it as a normal person and not as a corporate spokesperson. That's why everyone is writing all their thoughts on public web pages and asking for comments. They want to hear from you.

Find the Conversation

Every day, consumers are creating countless messages, blog posts, and emails that are full of word of mouth about businesses. Some of it, we hope, is about you.

As I suggested earlier, someone on your staff should be searching the web every morning for mentions of each of your major products. Make it part of the customer service team's job. Create a list of terms that you need to watch, including brands, product names, and key personnel.

First, use standard search engines to tell you when things are posted on mainstream websites and message boards. Next, use the free specialized search engines that look at the blogs. Feedster, Technorati, BlogPulse, and many others will tell you when something relevant has been posted. These tools are amazingly fast. You often know if something has been posted to a blog within minutes of its being written. These sites will also let you set up real-time notification to alert you when a new item containing your keywords has been posted.

For real-world conversations, you need to be on the lookout. You are probably not going to be there when most people are talking about you, so listening for offline word of mouth is a more passive activity. What you can do is be receptive and ready. Pay attention when customers call the company. Be alert wherever you might stumble on a conversation about you.

Reply and Respond

Reply and respond at every possible chance you have. There's only one thing you can do that's really wrong—fail to participate at all. You really don't have a choice. You must participate if you want any chance of influencing the conversation.

Feel free to be totally there. Make yourself available to talk to customers directly, anywhere they want to reach you.

Your ideas and input are welcome as long as they are relevant and in good taste. If bloggers didn't want feedback, they would be writing in paper diaries and stuffing them under their beds.

Here are my favorite ways to participate in the word of mouth conversation.

Thank People Who Say Nice Things About You. Leave a nice comment for the writers when you see a positive mention in a blog or message board. Tell them you appreciate it. Encourage them. You'll be amazed at what a little kindness does for your word of mouth.

You'll get a lot out of this. The original complimenter is more likely to become an active talker. Other people will notice that you're a cool company, and they'll talk about it. On most websites, your comment will automatically link back to your site, bringing you more visitors. And best of all, people will keep saying nice things if they feel warm and fuzzy about you and your stuff.

Fix Problems and Make People Happy. Look for people who have a problem or a complaint. Find a way to fix it, or at least offer to.

There is a reason they are complaining in public—they want your attention.

People will fall out of their chairs in shock when you do the right thing. It is so rare for companies to deal nicely with customers that any public, proactive effort becomes an instant word of mouth topic.

When you see a complaint or a gripe, post something like this: "Hi, I'm Andy from XYZ Company. I was reading your blog/message/website and was dismayed to hear that you couldn't get your Floobulator fixed. Try this: _____. Or email me, and I'll hook you up with the right people to take care of it."

You'll do more than make this one talker happy. You'll get every reader of that site gushing about you.

Of course, you should be doing the same extraordinary things in your offline customer service.

Anyone can make a mistake. How you deal with it determines what the word of mouth is going to be.

Just Join In

The best possible thing you can do?

Be a regular person and a positive contributor.

Every day, people are talking about stuff that relates to what you are selling. They care and they are interested. Everyone will be thrilled when someone with your expertise adds to the conversation.

My dad sells something called a TieYak. It's a very clever cable to lock up a kayak (which is harder than you think). It's a small business, and he can't spend much on advertising. But he does have a secret weapon: He knows way too much about kayaks.

There are 20 or so major message boards about kayaking. Every time he posts a topic, provides helpful advice, or just says hello, his posts all contain a link to the TieYak website. He doesn't need to sell or talk about the product, because people are smart enough to figure it out. His intelligent contributions to the conversation earn the respect that starts the word of mouth about his product.

THE RIGHT PEOPLE TO TAKE PART

Who should be participating? Anyone!

You don't need a formal word of mouth team. Involve anyone who enjoys being online, has a passion for what you do, and has the time to do it. Don't get too hung up on titles, either. This is a great way to get junior staff involved and give them an opportunity to become stars. I know a lot of successful executives who used their word of mouth smarts and initiative to get noticed and promoted at their companies.

Give your customer service reps access to the internet so they can get online and start looking for problems. Send your administrative assistant online to look for blogs and message boards where people are talking. Get everyone pumped up about the chance to get involved in great word of mouth.

I spoke with a national chain of gyms that plans to encourage all of its fitness trainers to blog for the company and become online customer advisors. It makes sense—the trainers share the same lifestyle and interests as potential talkers. Many of them are probably blogging anyway. Do you know if anyone on your staff is blogging?

Who Should Be Blogging?

Hint: it's not the PR or marketing folks.

Your best blogger will have true enthusiasm for your company and its products. A genuine love for the topic. The employee who wears the company shirt on weekends.

Participation never should stem from obligation; it should come from wanting to keep positive word of mouth going and from the knowledge that this is where positive word of mouth gets turned into action. It should be open to anyone who *wants* to do it but no one who *has* to it.

The bloggers already out there are interested in honest, open dialog and in being in the know. They'll be able to tell if you're serious about engaging in that kind of exchange.

For your blog to be credible, it's got to be real—honest, passionate, and plain-spoken. Blogging is how your company presents a human face, not its business one. Keep the marketing wordsmiths and the lawyers far away from the company blog. Anyone else who can speak honestly and normally should be welcome to do it.

Guideposts and Guardrails

Traditional marketing managers find this level of communications freedom really uncomfortable. It's hard enough to give up control of the message and let the customers run with it. It's sometimes harder to free your staff to go off and talk to those people without the controls of a formal marketing process.

So do what Intuit does—create what it calls "guideposts and guardrails." Give guidance and training for all interested employees who want to participate in the greater outside conversation. Teach your team the rules of the road and give them the instruction that they need, especially on the ethics rules. Set up strict guardrails that block forbidden behaviors.

Then you just need to let it happen.

If Microsoft can do it, anyone can. This formerly very tight-lipped company with formal marketing controls has opened up and encouraged 9,000 employees to start blogging—without supervision or control by the company. And each of those blogs is full of unfiltered comments from the public. The company has seen fantastic improvement in their reputation, consumer trust, and word of mouth, because they showed that they trust their team and the public to say what they feel.

GOOD MANNERS

You've heard plenty from me on the importance of honesty and ethics. Taking part is where you are most likely to make a mistake.

Good manners and a little common sense will keep you out of trouble. Step back if you think you're getting into a gray area. There's no good reason to go there (and lots of bad ones).

Never Sell

Taking part does not mean selling. Sticking a shameless sales pitch on a message board is wrong. It's just like spam. It's hated, and it will embarrass your company.

The purpose of participating is to keep your talkers talking about your topic. It's not to push products. Stick to the word of mouth topic, and stick to the reasons why people are talking. Share knowledge, add to the conversation, and make everyone feel appreciated and special.

Follow the Rules

Whether you are at a street fair or on a message board, there are always clear rules. Remember that you are on someone else's turf and you're a guest. Follow the rules wherever you are. Don't litter flyers all over the place. Don't post off-topic comments. Don't aggressively push your product. Just be a good citizen and respect the communities where the conversations are happening.

That may sound restrictive, but it's not. Imagine that on a message board for gardeners, a guy from a lawn mower store breaks the rules and posts a blurb about how great his products are and why they're better than the competition's. He'll probably get kicked off the message board. He'll definitely get attacked by the other posters for being an idiot. Not good word of mouth.

What he should do is talk about lawn problems and answer questions from gardeners who need advice on which products to use. People will appreciate the contribution and respect his willingness to share and his objectivity. They will also be able to figure out where the store is. That's how you get good word of mouth.

Say Who You Are

Nothing will turn people off more than you pretending to be something or someone you're not. And don't think for a minute you won't be spotted as a fake if you're out there masquerading as a consumer. As you learned earlier, this kind of shilling is a sure path to embarrassment.

Always disclose aggressively. It's not enough to just post your name. Say where you work and make it very obvious that you have something to gain by being in the conversation. You can start with something as simple as "I work for XYZ, but here's my personal take."

There's no need to pretend. Your affiliation with your company gives you *more* credibility, not less. As does your honesty.

THE POWER OF MAKING PEOPLE HAPPY

Grab a highlighter. An important idea is coming up.

Let's start with one of the key rules of thumb in word of mouth:

For every person whom a happy customer talks to . . .

- An unhappy customer tells five people.
- A formerly unhappy customer who is made happy tells 10 people.

Think about this for a minute. Finding a way to make unhappy people happy is worth 10 times more free word of mouth marketing than making them happy in the first place. It's probably a comment on the sad state of customer service these days that people are so surprised by being treated well that they run around telling everyone about it when it happens. But it's a great opportunity for you.

> **Big Idea: Fixing problems is the most powerful marketing you can do.**

The shock of getting an acknowledgment that their concerns matter immediately converts detractors into powerful talkers. These new talkers will be out there telling everyone about what a great company you are.

Give your team the freedom to make those people happy.

Follow the lead of Ritz-Carlton Hotels, which enables any employee to spend up to $2,000 instantly to make a customer happy. The hotel knows that instant satisfaction results in long-term customer spending—and extraordinary gestures result in immediate word of mouth.

Can you think of another use of marketing money or staff time that gets such a payback in terms of free advertising or customer acquisition?

Bob Parsons, president of domain name registrar GoDaddy.com, did a great job of setting the permanent record straight. He and his company were taken to task by the blogs for opting to spend $2.4 million on an ad that would run during the 2005 Super Bowl. Marketing expert John Moore blogged his view that it was a bad idea. Within 24 hours, Moore's comments started getting picked up by other blogs and getting responses, most of which were very negative about the company.

Instead of ignoring the online frenzy, however, Parsons replied the next day. He thanked people for their concerns and explained his reasons for going ahead with the ad—that the company had no debt and he was the sole investor; the money spent on the ad and the subsequent campaign would not take funding away from product development; and, as the founder, he really wanted to do it, even if it was silly. Throughout the following months, Parsons remained engaged, replying to others' comments and concerns.

His honesty and willingness to participate really struck people. Hundreds of comments were posted, most of which were positive. It is fascinating to follow the conversation and see how a little genuine participation turned people from attacking to publicly declaring their support for the company.

In what is now considered a defining incident, the risks of not taking part became apparent when you consider what Dell did (or, more accurately, didn't do) when it was criticized for poor customer service by Jeff Jarvis, a high-profile blogger. Jarvis posted some relatively mild complaints, and Dell didn't respond. The situation snowballed as more bloggers jumped on the story and piled on negative comments. The few replies that came from Dell's PR department seemed a bit clueless as to the significance of the situation. The bloggers persisted, daring the company to respond. By the time Dell did respond, it had lost significant credibility, and thousands of negative posts are still all over the web. The company had acted too late, and it paid a high price with a damaged permanent record and, undoubtedly, lost customers.

You have to take part.

DEALING WITH THE NEGATIVE

Probably the most common managerial objection I hear about word of mouth marketing is "What if someone says something bad?"

My indelicate response to this is, "So what?" Not knowing that people are saying bad things doesn't change the fact that they're saying them. Most likely, if people are saying something bad and you're not responding, the bad is only going to get worse.

Participating in the word of mouth conversation doesn't cause negative feedback. It gives you the tools to deal with the negative.

In fact, many of the things you should do to manage negative word of mouth are the exact same steps you should already be taking to earn good word of mouth.

How to Manage Negative Word of Mouth

1. *Know what people are saying.* Listen carefully so you catch any negative conversation early. I've said it throughout this book, but it's important: You should always know what is being said about your company. Don't get caught by surprise.

2. *Build credibility before you need it.* Nothing earns more credibility with bloggers than a company that is part of the blog community. The best thing you can do is to have genuine, nonspin blogs written by your team. But it is just as important to be a known participant in the blog world. Build a storehouse of goodwill in advance that you can benefit from when you need it.

3. *Show that you are listening.* Many bloggers are (pleasantly) surprised when they find out that a company is actually

reading what they write. Post a note when you read something you like. Post replies and comments when you see unfair criticism. Post an offer of help when you hear a complaint. Always identify your affiliation with your company and offer to solve any problems. In many cases, this is the most important thing you can do. Most negative conversation is actually a plea for assistance, and the negative stops when you solve the problem.

It's also important to remember that it's easier to talk badly about someone who you don't think is listening. When people find out that you are a responsive, accessible company, they are much more likely to reach out to you and work out problems instead of just attacking.

4. *Enable your hidden supporters.* Your hidden supporters are all those fans of your company who have never become talkers, but they like you and want to support you. Trust me, you have lots of friends like this.

They'll come out fighting when they hear that you've come under attack. This silent majority of supporters feels as though they are a part of your corporate family, and they will defend you like a member of the family. Think of them as talkers who need a really big reason to talk.

The only way you can rally these troops is if you're having an open conversation. There's no way for them to know you need their help if you hide from criticism, if you keep whatever's happening behind the scenes. Yes, if you're out in the open, you expose yourself to the good and the bad, but that is ultimately what's going to help you.

5. *Convert critics when you can.* You can't make all people happy all the time, but you sure can try. Treat critics like valuable customers and try to win them over with special attention. You'll get two great benefits. First, you'll have the story of a happy resolution posted on the critics'

websites. Second, as we know, converted critics become the most enthusiastic fans.

6. *Don't try to win.* In the end, don't expect to win every point in every debate. It's not possible. What you can do, however, is tell your side of the story. Write for the record. Post comments or entries in your own blog for posterity. Remember the permanent record, and write what you want history to see.

Many PR-trained executives find this kind of participation difficult because of the inherent lack of control over the situation. It's about learning to respond and participate instead of trying to plant and initiate. It's no longer about managing what other people say but about letting your own words speak for themselves. And it's about earning respect (but not necessarily agreement) from other people out there by showing that you know how to participate the right way.

Blogs are Upside Down

When you're replying to negative word of mouth online, it's important to remember that blogs are displayed in reverse chronological order. How you end the story is what people see first in the permanent record.

The final word counts most. We read blogs in the opposite order from which they were written, and that's how they are archived. A raucous blogosphere debate may have lots of criticism of your company. But if you resolve it well and make the blogger happy in the end, that final entry shows up at the top of the blog.

Newer posts show up first in search results. This means that the current conversation is much more visible than what happened even a few days earlier. When you reach out and resolve an online problem, the positive resolution is the first thing seen by new readers.

CHAPTER EIGHT

Tracking:
What Are People
Saying About You?

YOUR JOB:
LISTEN TO THE WORD OF MOUTH
AND LEARN FROM IT

We all want to know when someone is talking about us. Now we can.

When you track your word of mouth feedback, you can:

- find out who the talkers are
- learn which topics are working
- see if your tools are making a difference
- join in the conversation

Above all, you can learn what people are saying about your company and your stuff so you can make it better.

Companies spend more than $7 billion each year on market research. That's a lot of money to find out what people are saying.

The clunky part of the research process is getting people to tell you what they are really thinking. We have tools to pull ideas out of people, and the results are often messy. Focus groups can tell you what people think, but those opinions are often limited to the artificial environment of the focus group itself. Surveys can provide useful information, but they depend on your asking the right questions.

Then, all of sudden, something really crazy happened.

Millions of people started writing down everything they were thinking. Just like that, people are blogging, writing on message boards, and posting online reviews. And, as we know, much of that talk is about products and services.

So now we can just read it for ourselves. We don't have to hire companies to gather feedback for us. It turns out that the spontaneously written stuff on the web can be as useful as some of the formal research. Even better, what we find out on the web can be analyzed and used to project what people are saying in the offline world.

This makes word of mouth so much more than marketing. It's also your best market research tool.

Advanced Word of Mouth Measurement Techniques

A new market research specialty is growing up around this phenomenon, devoted to measuring word of mouth. Major market research firms and dozens of startups are building an impressive science of word of mouth measurement. They're able to analyze the conversations about a topic, brand, or product with incredible precision and speed.

These companies can identify and understand who the talkers are, what they are talking about, and trends in the conversation. They can also examine your customer database and determine which of your existing customers are likely to be your biggest talkers, or go out and find new talkers for you.

This book isn't going to get into the details of these advanced techniques, but I want you to know what is available.

The best place to find out more about how to do word of mouth measurement (and a great place to get free data) is the Word of Mouth Marketing Association's Research Blog at *www.womma.org/research*. That site will also link you to the best firms to hire if you want to do more advanced studies.

SIMPLE WAYS TO TRACK
WHAT PEOPLE ARE SAYING

I can't cram a full course on market research into this book. But I can help with some straightforward techniques that will give you a good intuitive sense of what people are saying about you, for little or no cost.

Now, as we know, most word of mouth is happening offline. But that part of it is harder to track and measure. (Most marketers aren't invited into the bedroom or kitchen to listen in on personal conversations.) The online conversation, however, is very public and easy to study.

Use Online Tracking Tools

You can find a surprising amount of useful information on the free websites mentioned earlier that search the blogs. In addition to showing you who's talking about you and what they're saying, these services can break down where the talkers are from, which sites they've come from, what they've looked at, what time of day they visited, and what they searched for to get there. They can also show you who's talking about you and organize the data with handy charts and graphs.

Some search engines will also tell you just how influential each of the talkers is. When you get a list of blog posts after searching in Technorati, it also tells you how many people are linking to that blog. More links means more influence.

Encourage Feedback

Do you really want to hear what people are saying? Then make it clear that you are listening and make it easy to give feedback. The best way to understand the word of mouth conversation is to get people to talk directly to you.

- Put up a really simple, easy-to-find feedback form on your website, and reply to the people who use it.

- Create an online message board where customers and future customers can talk to you and to each other. This works great for building word of mouth credibility, because every post, good or bad, is publicly visible. It shows that you have nothing to hide.

- Ask for comments offline also. Put postage-paid comment cards in every package and by the register. Instruct your salespeople to remind people to give feedback and tell them that you value what they say. Host a customer feedback meeting.

You'll get better results if you show that you are listening. Demonstrate that you care by putting the comments and your replies out in public. Print a selection of comments in your company newsletter. Post questions and answers on your website.

You can even create a system to specifically reward and recognize people for giving feedback. Amazon does it by labeling its most active participants as "Top 100" reviewers.

Listen to Tell-a-Friend Forms and Message Boards

Your tell-a-friend forms are more than tools for spreading word of mouth. They're also a powerful tool for tracking the conversation.

A good tell-a-friend form should send you a report every time it is used. That report will tell you quite a bit: what pages people are looking at when they feel motivated to tell a friend and how many people they are sending it to. The messages written by referrers are a great way to understand what people are saying to their friends about you. And, although you should never send unsolicited mail to the email addresses entered into the form (that's spamming), you can track how many referred email addresses become customers.

Tell-a-friend forms are also a great way to identify new topics. You never know which page on your website or item in your catalog will become a word of mouth topic. Keep that referral form on every single page, and watch it like a hawk. You know you have a hot topic when a bunch of people start sending referrals from the same page. Move that item to the home page and highlight it for the rest of your talkers.

You can get similarly good information from message boards or other online community tools.

Put Yourself Out There

Like everything else in life, things will pass you by if you're not alert and out there. There will be a lot more to listen to if people know you're involved and paying attention to them. When you're in chat rooms or message boards, say who you are and ask for feedback. You'll be amazed at how easy it is to get people talking back to you.

GM has figured this out. Vice Chairman Bob Lutz has a blog—a good one. It's not GM propaganda. It's about cars, and Lutz is clearly a car guy. His genuine enthusiasm shows. The most interesting reads are the comments posted after every piece. Simply put, the people posting on GM's blog pull no punches. The site gets hundreds of comments each week with lively interaction from people on the inside responding to real comments from the outside.

Some of it has to be difficult for Lutz and GM to read, although there are plenty of positive postings, but the value of this unsolicited, genuine feedback is incalculable. A conversation keeps going, giving participants huge amounts of information about GM and giving GM massive amounts of information about what customers think. The free research from the comments on the blog is worth as much as expensive research from focus groups.

As you get more active and involved, people will start to realize that your company is listening. They will start talking *to* you instead of *about* you. When that conversation gets good, then word of mouth starts to accelerate.

Sharing of Direct Mail

Direct mail is a useful tracking tool because the order forms usually have detailed codes that tell you who received each letter or catalog. Use this information to start looking for people who place orders who were *not* the original recipients. Those are word of mouth customers.

You can examine the trends in passed-along mailings to identify word of mouth patterns and new opportunities. Are you mailing to PR departments but getting orders from marketing managers? That shows there is clearly a word of mouth connection between the two departments.

Measure the Net Promoter Score

One very powerful, advanced measurement technique that you can do yourself is the Net Promoters Score, created by Fred Reichheld and discussed in his book *The Ultimate Question*. It starts with the fairly straightforward question, "Would you recommend this product to a friend?" and rates responses on a 10-point scale. This question works just as well for online or offline word of mouth.

If you subtract the percentage of negative responses from the percentage of positive ones (throwing out the neutral), you get your score. Basically, your word of mouth reputation is the number of people who respect you, less the number of people you annoy. To improve the score, you need to get fewer people to want to say negative things while earning more positive recommendations

At company after company, a better score usually means better word of mouth and higher profitability.

PUTTING VALUE ON
YOUR WORD OF MOUTH

By far the most common question I'm asked by big company executives is, "Can you put a specific value on word of mouth?" You can.

Unhide the Hidden Statistic

The first step is correctly identifying which customers are coming from word of mouth.

As I pointed out earlier, word of mouth has always been underreported—a hidden statistic—because most companies don't track it well. It's time to unearth it and give it its due.

Word of mouth needs to be clearly identified in your surveys and order forms. When you ask, "How did you hear about us?" be sure you're asking the right way. There should be a consistent, clear choice that indicates word of mouth. You won't be able to track the true impact of word of mouth if some say "from a friend" while others say "from a family member," "from a coworker," "from my doctor/lawyer/plumber/hairstylist," or "online." Tighten it up so that the answers are clear. "Online" might mean the Yellow Pages website or happy reviewers on a message board.

Do the same thing on your marketing reports—make sure there's a line for word of mouth there, too. When you list your sources of customers, be sure that word of mouth is properly reported alongside your other marketing campaigns.

Once you unhide this hidden statistic, you'll probably discover that you're getting a whole lot more word of mouth than you think.

Computing the Return on Investment of Word of Mouth

If you know the average lifetime value of your customers and you can estimate the number of customers you acquire through word of mouth, you can place a dollar value on your word of mouth marketing efforts.

This can also help you to put a value on your most active talkers. If you've identified who your best talkers are and know that they refer you to an average of six friends, and half of those people become customers, you can derive their value relative to customers who only refer you to two friends, and so on.

Agency ComBlu studied the talkers in a local Chicago wine store. They watched a customer who was a classic talker. He had no affiliation with the store; he just loved wine and loved helping people. While he was shopping, he would go up to confused shoppers and help them pick out the right wine. They measured whom he talked to and which wines were bought. The surprising result—this one talker generated more than $25,000 in annual sales for this single store.

Ultimately, this kind of knowledge can help you make smarter decisions about where to invest money in marketing (and nonmarketing) programs that drive word of mouth. Putting a value on something is the best way to justify investment in it.

Remember that customer service also drives word of mouth. This has profound implications for that part of your business. If you start to recognize customer service as not merely an expense but a way to create positive word of mouth, then you realize that spending on customer service generates a positive return on investment.

Earlier, I discussed the cost of bad customer service when multiplied by the power of word of mouth. It's important also to track the good side of the equation.

Find a way to follow which customer service moments are likely to generate a word of mouth referral (or even create an energized former critic who is now bringing in multiple referrals). Multiply these referrals by your average cost of acquiring a new customer. That's your formula for the value of great customer service.

AND IN
THE END . . .

Sixteen Sure-Thing, Must-Do, Awfully Easy Word of Mouth Marketing Techniques

Okay. You've read the book.

Now, before you forget it all, here's what you can do right now, today, to start a successful word of mouth campaign:

1. Look on the web for people talking about you.
2. Decide who will join those conversations. Start today.
3. Create a blog.
4. Make a new rule: Ask "Is this buzzworthy?" in every meeting.
5. Come up with one buzzworthy topic. Keep it simple.
6. Put something by your front door that will remind people to talk to a friend.
7. Let your talkers sign up for a private newsletter.
8. Pick one easy way to track word of mouth.
9. Put a tell-a-friend form on every page of your website.
10. Put a special offer in an easily forwardable email.
11. Add a small gift and a word of mouth tool to every package you sell.
12. Have a private sale for your talkers.
13. Apologize for mistakes and solve problems fast.
14. Partner with a charity.
15. Do something unexpected.
16. Be nice.

Do something worth talking about!

Choose to Be Good

Word of mouth marketing is about being good to people.

Real people will talk about you when they like you, your stuff, and the things that you do. The word of mouth that they create is far more powerful than all the advertising in the world.

It's a wonderful thing: Happy people grow your business.

In the end, it's much more fun to go to work each day at a respected company that is honest, fun, and treats people well.

It's also a great way to become a successful business.

You can make that happen.

Afterword

YET ANOTHER TOP 10
BY GUY KAWASAKI

I just loved this book. (Word of mouth marketing is so Macintosh way-ish that I felt right at home reading it.) I've never written an afterword, but Seth did the foreword so this was all that was left for me to do.

Here are the ten ideas, stories, and recommendations that I liked most in this book:

1. Companies should hire a customer service rep to cruise the internet looking for kudos and complaints. When the rep finds kudos, he should thank the person. When the rep finds complaints, he should get the problem fixed.

2. Commerce Bank has a free change-counting machine in its branches that anyone can use. Beats the hell out of the machines in markets that take 7 percent.

3. A study by the Verde Group showed that people who heard about a bad shopping experience are less likely to go to the same store than the person who actually had the bad experience.

4. The most powerful word of mouth advocates might be the customers who have done business with you only once so far. They are the most excited; repeat customers are probably used to the great product/service.

5. The Prostate Net contacted 50,000 barbers to talk to their clients about prostate cancer detection and prevention.

6. Incentives and rewards are likely to reduce word of mouth advertising because motivation becomes suspect. You can't "buy" word of mouth advertising.

7. The Wynn Las Vegas hotel gave free rooms to cabbies to generate word of mouth advertising via this very influential part of the transportation infrastructure.

8. Henkel Consumer Adhesives, the manufacturer of Duck Tape, sponsors a contest for college scholarships called "Stuck at Prom."

9. A word of mouth campaign brought back *Family Guy* from the dead (that is, cancellation).

10. Zappos has a one-year, no-questions-asked return policy for shoes. This boggles my mind although I've never seen my wife return anything to them.

Someday I hope to read about your kick-butt idea in a book like this!

Guy Kawasaki
Blog.guykawasaki.com